1994 WORLD CHAMPION SAN FRANCISCO 49ERS
SUPER BOWL XXIX

SF

COOKIN' WITH

CHAMPIONS

★ ★

WINNING RECIPES
— FROM THE —
SAN FRANCISCO 49ERS

WITH NUTRITIONAL OPTION PLAYS | BY THE AMERICAN CANCER SOCIETY

PRODUCED BY

Helen Mendel, CMD

PHOTOGRAPHED BY

Jeff Bayer

WRITTEN BY

Richard Weiner

DESIGN

Tharp Did It

For Gina, whose bravery and smile I remember most. To my Papa Dave, a remarkable man, I miss you.
Family and friends, Marybeth, Maureen, Jackie, Wendy, Michael, and my ACS family,
thank you for encouraging me. And, for all the ACS volunteers who give their time and talent. – H.M.

COOKIN' WITH CHAMPIONS
STARTING LINEUP

PRODUCER
Helen Mendel, CMD

DESIGNERS
of Tharp Did It :
Susan Craft
Debra Naeve
Rick Tharp

PHOTOGRAPHER
Jeff Bayer
(except where noted)

WRITER
Richard Weiner

FLIP BOOK
ILLUSTRATOR
Max Seabaugh, MAX

EDITOR
Ralph Hendrickson

TYPOGRAPHER
FotoComp

**NUTRITIONAL
OPTION PLAYS**
Jenifer Peale

**PRODUCTION
ASSOCIATE**
Graphic Arts West

**RECIPE
CONSULTANT**
Judy Hobbs

PRINTER
Jim Otis,
Bay Area Press

COVER

PHOTOGRAPHY
Stan Cacitti

STYLING
Judy Hobbs

**DIGITAL
SPECIAL EFFECTS**
Mike Haynes

**DESIGN &
ART DIRECTION**
Rick Tharp

"SPECIAL TEAMS" PLAYERS

Marilyn Broussard
Jamie David
Pat Felts
Tom Gates M.D.
Robert Gengler Esq.
Lori Grbac
Dwight Hicks

Marilyn Jackson
Mike McDevitt
Jack Otis, GAC
Julie Otis
Michael Rohde
John Simmons M.D.
Gaylord Walker

ACKNOWLEDGEMENTS

Lisa DeBartolo
49ers Foundation

Maggie Valencia
49er Organization

American Cancer Society / California Division Inc.

For additional copies of this book call 1.800.ACS.2345

**AMERICAN
CANCER
SOCIETY**

Not all recipes have been professionally tested.

This book was printed on Simpson's Silverado Book. The cover was printed on Federal's Carolina Cover.

STEVE YOUNG PUNCHES OVER THE GOAL LINE FOR A CRUCIAL SCORE IN THE 49ER 1994 NFC CHAMPIONSHIP GAME VICTORY OVER DALLAS.

F O R W A R D

When I was asked to write the forward for Cookin' With Champions, my first reaction was to have my eldest daughter Lisa describe how vital a fund-raising vehicle this is for both the 49ers Foundation and the American Cancer Society. Lisa, after all, has been in the trenches the past three years while running the 49ers Foundation, which helps support numerous charitable groups.

Studies show that about 10 million Californians have cancer and that over the years this disease will strike approximately three in four families in the state. Doctors seem to be closing in on the genes they believe to be at the core of most cancers. Yet, for those sitting in hospital rooms receiving chemo- or radiation therapy, time is not waiting. They tell me approximately 52,685 people in California will die from cancer in 1996. This is why even the smallest donation, such as the purchase of this book, can make a difference.

The 49ers have been blessed with the greatest fans in the National Football League. You have supported us through numerous changes, crucial losses—and, thankfully, been able to celebrate with us after five Super Bowl victories. By purchasing this limited edition book not only can you take home an exclusive look at the players' lifestyles, but you can make a difference in the biggest game of all—life.

When the 50,000 copies of *Cookin' With Champions* are sold, nearly a million dollars will have been raised and divided between the American Cancer Society and the 49ers Foundation. That's quite a difference you are making just by purchasing this book for yourself, a friend or a family member.

Moreover, the American Cancer Society is offering nutritional pointers throughout these pages, which, as you probably know, translates into one of the first keys for a healthy lifestyle. I, too, am consciously trying to eat the proper foods to promote health and prevent illness.

Of course, my lovely wife Candy is the world-class chef in our family. Me? I do the grill or barbecue thing. So, we'll be combing these pages just like you to see how Steve Young prepares cheesecake, or what makes Jerry Rice's Flash 80 Rice so tasty. I can heartily recommend George Seifert's Smoked Salmon Quiche.

When I look at this book, I'll sit back and smile knowing the effort that was put into it by so many caring people. We can make a difference well beyond the football field. There's no greater feeling than that in life.

God Bless,

Edward DeBartolo, Jr.
Owner, San Francisco 49ers

T H E   L I N E U P

CONTENTS

The game has changed. On the field, football players are bigger, stronger, faster than ever. Their salaries dwarf not only those of their predecessors, but also those of most of their fans. Because of this, it appears as though the gap between athletes and the public is wider than the holes ripped in opponents' defenses by 49er linemen. ❧ Until now. ❧ *Cookin' With Champions* is one of those rare projects in which athletes and the public can join hands to make a difference. Read on, and you'll find hope in the modern athlete who has been stereotyped as part of a "me first" generation. ❧ Most followers of football know about the San Francisco 49ers and their unprecedented attainment of five Super Bowl trophies. But only those in area hospitals or in need can share the stories of how 49er players have visited them or called with offers of support or simply to talk. Most players prefer to keep their contributions private. They give of themselves out of a desire to help those less fortunate. The joy is in the giving. ❧ They say the 49er Faithful "eats up" anything involving their team. Well, here's something they can get their teeth into: a book of recipes, comments, nutritional hints and other tips from the National Football League's most successful team. ❧ The profits from this limited edition book will benefit the American Cancer Society and the

49ers Foundation. It was compiled by an all-star team ranging from New York to Maui, picked for their individual expertise— and personal experiences with cancer. 🏈 All the players, from current stars Jerry Rice and Steve Young to Hall of Famers such as the entire "million dollar backfield" of Y. A. Tittle, Joe Perry, Hugh McElhenny and John Henry Johnson, have donated time. Again, that is nothing new for most of these players. 🏈 What's new is how close cancer researchers are getting in their fight against the disease. The American Cancer Society, for instance, awarded over $90 million for research in 1994. With that financial backing, scientists have come close to discovering genes which may be the leading cause of common cancers found in the human body. They've also successfully taken on the tobacco industry, which continues to promote cancer causing products. In California alone, the American Cancer Society has 130,000 volunteers. 🏈 "My father's father had cancer, my mom's mom had cancer," Lisa DeBartolo said. "That gives this book a double meaning for me. I have been touched by cancer in my life and for the past three years my life has been the 49ers Foundation, an organization which raises money for community groups and services." 🏈 Go into the locker room and you'll find players with stories about friends or relatives who have been stricken by cancer. One of the most inspiring stories involves All-Pro tackle Harris Barton and his late father, Paul. Harris has never been the vocal type. He always showed up to work first, worked as long or harder than anyone else, did his job on the field and shied away from interviews. Yet, when his father was diagnosed with cancer, Harris set out on a mission to help create awareness of the disease. His United Way commercials for the American Cancer Society still bring a tear to anyone's eye. 🏈 "I think that the public, when they look at athletes," Barton says, "see a guy running around on the field and not giving a lot back to the community. The reality is a lot of players, on their days off and during the offseason, spend time in areas that deserve more acknowledgment. 🏈 "Certainly, I've dedicated a lot to the study and cure of cancer because of my father's death." Barton said, "It's an important issue. Everybody that you know will someday be affected by cancer. That needs to stop." 🏈 The players wish they could reach every cancer patient in the Bay Area. Kevin Lewis, a former 49ers cornerback, used to ask a different player each week to the Stanford Children's Hospital—until he got to a point where players were lining up to go with him. 🏈 One of the best stories which tells what Steve Young stands for came a few years back when he learned of a young cancer patient who happened to be one of his biggest fans. He initiated a telephone relationship with the woman while she endured 18 months of chemotherapy, often calling her from hotels while the team was out of town. When he learned about what would be her last visit to the team's complex, he came off the practice field, marched straight through the locker room and out to the lobby. There he sat and spoke with her in full gear. Unfortunately, there are too many cancer patients to be touched by so few players. There-in lies the beauty of this book. There was a lot of love and care put into the following pages, even though the players were busy defending their Super Bowl title.

Call it an insert to the gameplan of life. Nutrition is just one aspect, but it may be the most vital. Appropriately this book was fine-tuned by Jenifer Peale, a nutritionist with the American Cancer Society. You'll see her option plays suggesting ways to enhance the nutritional value of a recipe without compromising taste. You'll also learn what some of your 49er heroes eat during game days. Certainly, these tips are different from the training table diets used by the dominant Green Bay Packers of the 1960s. Their coach Vince Lombardi had them eat steak and eggs for breakfast before they played. Yes, the game has changed. In this case, it's for the better.

IRS

ADMINISTRATION

"Mr. D" bought the team in 1977 and soon earned the reputation as the most generous owner in NFL history. Because of his ability to treat employees properly, the 49ers became a model franchise, capturing an unprecedented five Super Bowl titles.

EDWARD J. DEBARTOLO, JR.

Marinara Sauce

Serves 6

S T A R T E R S

1 can (12 oz.) · · · · · · · · · · · · · · **tomato paste**	
4 cans (28 oz.) · · · · · · · · **whole tomatoes**	
run through blender	
1 · · · · · · · · · · · · · **medium onion,** chopped	
4 cloves · · · · · · · · · · · · · · · **garlic,** chopped	

1 to 1-1/2 Tblsp. extra virgin olive oil

1 lb. · **pasta**
any kind

handful · **parsley**

2 Tblsp. · **sugar**

G A M E P L A N

In a 6-quart pot sauté chopped garlic in oil. Add chopped onion and cook until soft and transparent. Add the tomato paste and stir until well mixed. Add sugar and parsley, cook slowly for approximately 1-1/2 hours. Stirring occasionally. Spoon over pasta and serve immediately.

A U D I B L E

For spicier flavor add 1 tsp. of crushed red pepper while the sauce is simmering.

15

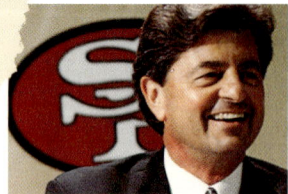

Fast became one of the most influential executives in the NFL, sweeping Executive of Year honors after the 1994–95 season. Initially moved from Youngstown, Ohio, to help shape the 49ers for the budget-concerned 90s; now could write book on mastering the salary cap.

CARMEN POLICY

Cioppino
[negotiated from wife Gail]

Serves 8

S T A R T E R S

1/3 cup · **olive oil**	
1 cup · · · · · · · · · · · **green onion,** chopped	
1 cup · · · · · · · · · · · · · · · · · **onion,** chopped	
1 cup · · · · · · · · · **green pepper,** chopped	
4–6 cloves · · · · · · · · · · · **garlic,** crushed	
2 cans (1 lb. 12 oz.) · · · · · · · · · · · **tomatoes**	
1 can (16 oz.) · · · **Contadina Italian style tomato sauce**	
1 can (8 oz.) · · · · · **regular tomato sauce**	
1 can (6 oz.) · · · · · · · · · · · · **tomato paste**	

1 can (6 oz.) · **water**

2 cups · · · · · · · · · · · · · · · · · **dry red wine**

1/4 cup · · · · · · · · · **fresh parsley,** chopped
fresh basil, oregano leaves

1 Tblsp. · **sugar**

· · · · · · · · · · · · · **parmesan cheese,** grated

· · · · · · · · · · · **fresh shrimp, crab, lobster, littleneck clams and scallops**

2 lbs. · **linguine**

17

G A M E P L A N

In a large saucepan sauté onion, green onion, green pepper and garlic in olive oil for 10 minutes. Add tomatoes, Italian style sauce, regular sauce, tomato paste, water and wine. Bring to a boil and then lower temperature. Add parsley, basil, oregano and sugar. Simmer for at least 2 hours. Add fresh seafood to the sauce during the last 15 to 20 minutes of cooking time (do not over cook). Cook linguine according to package directions. Cover linguine with sauce, sprinkle with parmesan cheese and evenly distribute seafood.

A U D I B L E

Sauce is best when made a day or two in advance. The seafood must be bought fresh and cooked into the sauce the day it is served. If sauce is made in advance, re-heat and add the seafood at that time.

Made the single most important catch in franchise history (see page 100-101), leaping high in the air to snag the conference championship away from Dallas in 1981. Now in charge of daily operations for the team after a stellar playing career. His first draft? Traded up to land J. J. Stokes in the first round.

DWIGHT CLARK

Summer Chicken

Serves 5

STARTERS

10	chicken breast halves, boneless, skinless
1	Mallard's Ginger Stir-Fry Sauce and Marinade
6	ears of white or yellow corn, cut off cob and use liquid
1 each	yellow, green and red peppers, cut into strips
8–10	medium mushrooms, sliced

1	small onion
1 can (4 1/2 oz.)	chicken broth and water
1/4 cup	milk
1/4 cup	olive oil
2	garlic cloves, minced

SUBSTITUTES

1 can · low-sodium fat-free chicken broth

GAMEPLAN

Marinate chicken breasts at least one hour in Mallard's Marinade. Prepare corn and place in a medium saucepan with milk, set aside. Prepare remaining vegetables. In a large, deep skillet sauté onions, garlic and mushrooms in oil until soft. Throw in peppers for the last 3 minutes. Remove vegetables and set aside in a bowl. Next brown the chicken breasts 5 at a time. Return all the chicken to the pan and drizzle the top with more marinade. Add chicken broth and water to the skillet. Simmer until chicken is done and liquid is reduced. While chicken simmers, heat corn for 10 minutes. Throw in the remaining vegetables for the last few minutes just to reheat. Cover the bottom of the plate with vegetables, place the chicken on top and drizzle everything with the sauce from the pan. All the ingredients can be adjusted to personal taste.

OPTION PLAY

Try not to use excessive oil to brown breasts. Use the low-sodium fat-free chicken broth.

19

Once the behind-the-scenes defensive genius behind the 49ers' first three Super Bowls, promoted from coordinator to head coach in 1989 and immediately won another title. Has the best winning percentage of any active coach in the NFL. Led the team to two Super Bowl titles and three NFC title games in first six years.

GEORGE SEIFERT
Smoked Salmon Quiche

Serves 6

STARTERS

1	uncooked pie shell
1/4 cup	mushrooms, sliced
1/4 cup	green onions, sliced
1/4 cup	tomatoes, chopped
1/4 cup	green pepper
1/4 lb.	cream cheese
4	eggs
1 cup	milk
1/2 tsp.	salt
1 tsp.	pepper
	nutmeg to taste
1/4 lb.	smoked salmon

SUBSTITUTES

2	whole eggs or 4 egg whites
1 cup	1% milk

GAMEPLAN

Sauté mushrooms, green onions, tomatoes and green pepper in butter. Cream the cheese and add eggs one at a time. Add milk and seasonings to egg mixture. In uncooked pie shell place the salmon and sautéed vegetables. Pour egg mixture over salmon and vegetables, bake at 350°F for 15 minutes. Reduce heat to 300°F and bake 45 minutes longer.

OPTION PLAY

Olive oil for butter. To make this recipe low-fat use 2 whole eggs and 4 egg whites. Also use 1% milk.

21

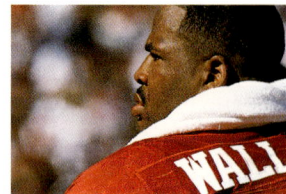

74 Drafted out of Auburn as part of the stellar Class of 1986, has become one of the most dominant left tackles in the league. Has a reputation of literally shutting down top opponents during big games, often posting "shutouts" by keeping top sack specialists off the tackle charts.

STEVE WALLACE
Grandma's Meat Loaf

Serves 8

STARTERS

1 cup	**onion,** freshly chopped
1 Tblsp.	**oil**
2	**eggs,** beaten
1 cup	**red wine or water**
2 lbs.	**lean ground beef**
3 cups	**carrot,** grated

2 Tblsp. each	**prepared mustard and chili powder**
2 tsp. each	**salt, garlic powder and Worcestershire sauce**
1/2 cup	**parsley,** chopped
1/2 cup	**chili sauce**

25

GAMEPLAN

Sauté onion in oil until soft. In a large bowl combine onion with all remaining ingredients except the 1/2 cup chili sauce. Mix until well combined. On a lightly oiled baking pan form a loaf of equal thickness. Spoon the reserved sauce over top. Bake in middle of 350°F oven for 1 hour and 15 minutes, until done.

OPTION PLAY

Use half beef and half ground lean turkey meat. 1 teaspoon of salt should suffice with the other seasoning.

AUDIBLE

Makes a great sandwich the next day.

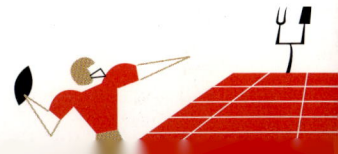

76 Signed a multi-million dollar contract as a free agent from Denver. Immediately proved his worth by stepping into the starting lineup during his first season with the 49ers, in 1995-96, when coaches said he was too good to keep on the bench.

KIRK SCRAFFORD

Beef Stroganoff

Serves 4

STARTERS

12 oz.	beef tenderloin or sirloin steak
1 Tblsp.	butter
1-1/2 cups	fresh mushrooms
1	medium onion, cut into wedges
1 clove	garlic, minced
2 cups	water
1 pkg. (4 oz.)	dried mafalde or ribbon noodles
2 tsp.	beef bouillon granules
1/4 tsp.	pepper
1 carton (8 oz.)	dairy sour cream
2 Tblsp.	all-purpose flour
1 Tblsp.	snipped parsley

SUBSTITUTES

low-fat sour cream

GAMEPLAN

Trim fat from the beef. Thinly slice beef across the grain into bite size strips. In a large skillet cook and stir meat in butter until brown. Remove meat from skillet, set aside. Add mushrooms, onion and garlic to skillet. Cook until vegetables are tender, stirring occasionally. Stir in water, pasta, bouillon granules and pepper. Bring to a boil, reduce heat. Cover and simmer about 12 minutes or till pasta is tender, stirring frequently. Blend together sour cream and flour. Stir sour cream mixture and parsley into the pasta mixture. Return beef strips to the skillet. Cook until bubbly, stirring gently. Cook and stir for one minute more.

OPTION PLAY

Cut down on the fat intake by using low-fat sour cream instead of regular sour cream.

27

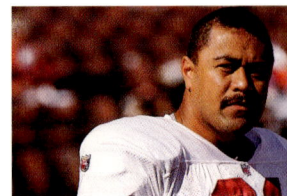

61 The elder statesman on the 49ers' roster, in terms of his stay with the team (since 1983). Overcame foot injuries at the start of his career to become a stalwart on the line during the team's last three Super Bowls. A legend in his native Hawaii, where he returned as a member of the Pro Bowl in 1994.

JESSE SAPOLU
Chicken Hekka

Serves 8–10

STARTERS

3 lbs. · · · · · · · · · · · · · · · · · · · **chicken,** cut up

1 stalk · **gobo**
(burdock root), cleaned and sliced

2 · · · · · · · · · · · · · · · · · · **large onions,** sliced

1 can · · · · · · · · · · **bamboo shoots,** sliced

5 · · · · · · · · · · · · · **shitake mushrooms,**
soaked and sliced (save liquid)

1 pkg. · · · · · · · · · · · · · · · · · · · **long rice**
soaked or cooked in boiling water, cut in halves

1/2 block · **tofu**
(bean curd), cut into 1 inch cubes

greens for hekka · · · · **carrots, lettuce,
scallions and watercress**

BROTH FOR COOKING

1/3 cup · **soy sauce**

1/3 cup · · · · · · · · · · · · · · · · · · **rice vinegar**

5 Tblsp. · · · · · · · · · · · · · · · · · · **raw sugar**

1-1/2 cups · · · · · · · · · · · · · **mushroom water**

1 tsp. · · · · · · · · · · · · · **Hawaiian salt** (rock salt)

29

GAMEPLAN

Combine broth ingredients, cook and bring to a boil. Put into a container and set aside. Stir-fry chicken pieces in margarine until pinkness is gone. Add gobo, bamboo shoots, and mushrooms. Cook in covered pot. After 10 minutes, add broth and cook covered. Add onions. After another 10 minutes, add long rice and tofu. Cook until tofu and long rice have soaked up the seasoning. Just before serving, add carrots, lettuce, scallions and watercress. Cook 1 to 2 minutes longer or until the greens are limp.

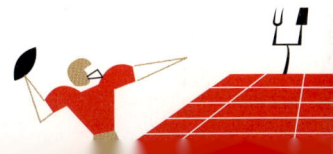

79 Known for obsessive film- and weight-room study, protects blind side of his left-handed quarterback so well he has been a perennial All-Pro selection since joining the team in 1987 out of North Carolina. So agile for his size, most other teams would play him at guard.

HARRIS BARTON

"On the Double" Sloppy Joes

Serves 6–8

STARTERS

2-1/2 cups	onions, chopped
1 Tblsp.	oil
1-1/2 lbs.	lean ground beef
1 cup	ketchup
1 Tblsp.	cider vinegar
1 Tblsp.	Worcestershire sauce
2 tsp.	prepared mustard
2 tsp.	celery seed
1 tsp.	sugar
1/2 tsp.	salt
1/2 tsp.	pepper
	toasted buns

SUBSTITUTES

1 Tblsp.	olive oil
1-1/2 lbs.	lean ground sirloin

GAMEPLAN

Sauté onions in oil over medium heat for 5 minutes. Increase heat, add the ground beef stirring to break up large pieces. Cook until beef is brown. Add all remaining ingredients, mix well. Cover and simmer for 10 minutes on low heat. Serve in or over toasted buns.

OPTION PLAY

For less fat and calories, use olive oil and ground sirloin.

31

84 Owner of the best hands of any NFL tight end, this local product (Santa Clara University, Leland High in San Jose) has become perennial All-Pro as Steve Young's most comfortable target. To think the Pittsburgh Steelers allowed him to leave after drafting him in 1986.

BRENT JONES

Turkey Tacos
[pass from wife Dana]
Serves 6

S T A R T E R S

2 lbs. · · · · · · **lean ground turkey breast**

1 pkg. · · · · · · · · · · **non-fat flour tortillas**

10 · · · · · · · **small Roma dried tomatoes,** diced small

1 head · · · · · · · · · · · · · **lettuce,** chopped fine

1 bunch · · · · · · **green onions,** chopped fine

2 pkg. · · · · · · · · · · · · · · · · · **taco seasoning**

1 jar · · · · · · · · · · · · · · · **your favorite salsa**

· · · · · **low-fat cheddar and jack cheese,** grated to taste

G A M E P L A N

Tortillas: either microwave for softness or lightly brown in skillet until crunchy. Cook turkey in Dutch oven with 1 cup of water until all the pink is gone, then drain. Return to the Dutch oven adding seasoning mix and heat thoroughly. Add green onions and cook an additional 10 minutes. Serve tomatoes and cheese in separate dishes. Top with your favorite salsa.

A U D I B L E

This is a healthy recipe "as is."

33

82 Still the most dangerous receiver in football after the catch. Says the 1995-96 season will be his last - this after joining the 49ers in 1986 out of Delaware State. Was named to the NFL's all-time Super Bowl roster as a punt returner. Perfect complement to Jerry Rice.

JOHN TAYLOR

Golden Pound Cake
[pass from wife Elayne]
Serves 8

STARTERS

2 cups	unsalted butter
3 cups	cake flour
1 cup	heavy cream or milk

2 Tblsp.	vanilla extract
8	large eggs
3-1/2 cups	white sugar

GAMEPLAN

Preheat oven to 350°F. Use electric mixer to beat butter until soft. Gradually add sugar and continue beating until light and fluffy. Add eggs and beat well. When they are blended, add flour, 1 cup at a time. Stir in cream and vanilla. Spread some butter and flour on a 9 x 4 1/2 inch loaf pan. Transfer the batter to the loaf pan and bake until golden brown.

AUDIBLE

Very rich. Don't eat too much!

80 Sets tone for 49ers both in work ethic and desire to keep winning. Has scored more touchdowns than any player in NFL history (see page 132). Considered the best conditioned player in the league. Nine-time Pro Bowl selection has starred in three Super Bowls. Joined team from tiny Mississippi State in 1985 when other teams thought he was too slow.

JERRY RICE
"Flash 80" Rice

Serves 8

STARTERS

I cup	long grain white rice
1-3/4 cups	chicken broth or canned chicken soup
3/4 cup	water
4 Tblsp.	butter
1/2 cup	red or green peppers, chopped
2 stalks	celery, chopped

2	small tomatoes, chopped
2	green onions, chopped
6	stuffed green olives, sliced

SUBSTITUTES

4 Tblsp.	margarine
1 cup	brown rice

GAMEPLAN

Chop the vegetables into small pieces. Using a 3 quart casserole dish, brown the rice in a microwave for 5 minutes or until rice is as brown as you like it. Stir the rice often with a wooden spoon. Bring 1-1/2 cups of chicken broth/soup to a boil, add the hot broth and butter to the rice mixture. Cover and cook 8 minutes, stirring twice. Add remaining 1/4 cup broth/soup, plus 3/4 cup water to rice. Cover and cook 5 more minutes, stirring occasionally. Using a fork quickly fluff vegetables into cooked rice. Let stand covered for 10 minutes before serving.

OPTION PLAY

Use margarine instead of butter for less fat. Brown rice may be substituted for white rice. Brown rice contains more vitamins, minerals and fiber.

37

8 Simply the best and most exciting passer in the league—and the most dominant running quarterback in NFL history (see page 3). Consensus league and Super Bowl MVP after 1994-95 season. Led NFL in passing unprecedented fourth consecutive season. Acquired in trade from Tampa Bay in 1987.

STEVE YOUNG

Cherry Cheesecake

Serves 6–8

STARTERS

1 .... graham cracker crust

1 pkg. .... cream cheese

1 can .... sweetened condensed milk

1/3 cup .... lemon juice

1 can .... cherry pie filling

39

GAMEPLAN

Mix cream cheese and sweetened condensed milk until smooth. Add lemon juice and blend. Pour blended mixture into graham cracker crust and chill. Before serving, spread the cherry filling over the pie.

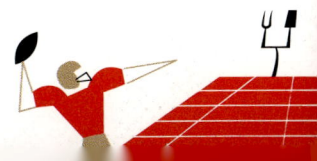

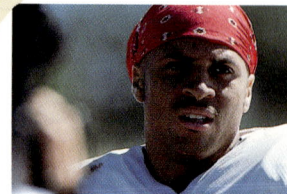

20 His rise to the starting lineup enabled the team to let Ricky Watters sign with the Philadelphia Eagles. Developed work-horse reputation as Bay Area prep standout and at University of Oregon. Reminds some of young Roger Craig.

DEREK LOVILLE

Chicken and Swiss Cheese

Serves 4

STARTERS

4 ················· large chicken breasts

4 ········ large slices of Swiss cheese

1 8oz. can ···· cream of chicken soup

1/3 soup can ·············· white wine

1/2 pkg. ············· Pepperidge Farm
stuffing mix

1/2 stick ························· butter

GAMEPLAN

Place chicken in pan (season to taste). Mix soup and wine together. Pour liquid over chicken. Place Swiss cheese on each piece of chicken. Melt butter and pour over stuffing. Cook at 350°F for approximately 55 minutes.

OPTION PLAY

You could cut down a little on the fat by using lower-fat products, but this is essentially a very high-fat dish.

41

40 Was branded with the nickname "Bar None" during training camp of rookie season in 1994 out of Florida State—and immediately backed up claim that he would be the best fullback in the league. Something of a '90s version/combination of Roger Craig and Tom Rathman.

WILLIAM FLOYD

Fish House Chowder

Makes 3 quarts

S T A R T E R S

1/2 lb.	**bacon,** diced
3	**large baking potatoes**
5 cups	**water**
1-1/2 tsp.	**salt**
1	**medium onion,** chopped
3 Tblsp.	**flour**
1-1/2 cups	**milk**
1 cup	**sour cream**

1/4 cup	**prepared mustard**
1 Tblsp.	**caraway seeds**
3/4 tsp.	**white pepper**
2 lbs.	**firm white fish** (halibut, cod), boneless
1/2 cup	**parsley,** chopped
	lemon wedges

43

G A M E P L A N

Cook bacon until crisp. Drain, reserving 3 tablespoons drippings. Peel and dice potatoes into 3/4 inch cubes. In large soup kettle bring potatoes to a boil. Reduce heat, cover and simmer until just tender, about 10 minutes. In medium saucepan sauté onion in reserved bacon drippings until soft. Stir in flour until smooth. Stirring, add milk and cook until sauce boils and thickens. Remove from heat. Whisk in sour cream, mustard, caraway seeds, pepper and remaining 1/2 tsp. salt. Cover and warm. Coarsely chop fish. Add fish to potatoes and cook 5 minutes longer. Stir sour cream, mustard mixture into chowder. Add bacon and parsley. Stir until combined. Heat through and serve.

BART OATES

49er Fudge Cake
[recovered from wife Michelle]
Serves 12–16

S T A R T E R S

1 cup	**butter**
4 Tblsp.	**Hershey's cocoa**
1 cup	**water**
2 cups	**flour,** sifted
2 cups	**sugar**
1/2 tsp.	**salt**
2	**eggs**
1/2 cup	**buttermilk or whole milk**

1/2 tsp.	**baking soda**
2 tsp.	**vanilla**

F R O S T I N G

1/2 cup	**butter**
4 Tblsp.	**cocoa**
6 Tblsp.	**milk**
1 tsp.	**vanilla**
I pkg. (12oz.)	**powdered sugar**

44

G A M E P L A N

Bring butter, Hershey's cocoa and water to boil. Pour this mixture over the flour, sugar and salt. Mix until smooth. Add eggs, buttermilk or whole milk, baking soda and 2 teaspoons of vanilla. Mix all ingredients. Bake at 375°F for 30 minutes in floured 13 x 9 inch pan. Prepare frosting by boiling butter, cocoa and milk together. Remove from heat and add 1 teaspoon vanilla. Mix, then add powdered sugar. Spread over cake while cake is still warm.

O P T I O N   P L A Y

Don't eat too much!

66 Once a feared rival with the New York Giants, joined the 49ers last season and re-united with his college quarterback and fellow lawyer, Steve Young. Known for rarely missing games, was key link to rebuilt offensive line during drive for Super Bowl XXIX.

CHRIS DALMAN
Pacific Tuna Tetrazzini

Serves 6–8

STARTERS

1 cup	**onion,** minced
2 large cloves	**garlic,** pressed
2 Tblsp.	**olive oil**
1/2 tsp. each pepper, salt and **thyme,** crumbled	
4 Tblsp. (1/4 cup)	**flour**
1 to 1-1/2 cup	**milk**
1 can (14 1/2 ounces)	**chicken broth**

1 cup	**parmesan cheese,** grated, divided
1 cup	**frozen peas,** thawed
1 jar (4 oz.)	**pimiento pieces**
1/2 cup	**parsley,** finely chopped
1/2 pound	**spaghetti,** cooked
2 cans (7 oz.)	**white tuna,** drained

45

GAMEPLAN

Sauté onion, garlic and mushrooms in olive oil until onion is soft. Stir in thyme, salt, pepper and flour. Mix well. Over medium heat slowly add milk and chicken broth stirring until smooth. Bring sauce to a boil, stirring until thickened. Heat through. Mix cooked spaghetti and tuna with sauce and 1/2 cup cheese. Turn into a shallow, oiled 3 quart casserole. Sprinkle with remaining 1/2 cup cheese. Bake, uncovered, in 375°F oven until hot and bubbly, about 30 to 45 minutes.

OPTION PLAYS

You can reduce the fat in this dish by using 1% milk, water packed tuna and half the oil and cheese.

67 When the 49ers head into the next century, is expected to be stalwart on the offensive line. Versatile interior lineman was drafted out of Stanford in 1993.

ROD MILSTEAD

Smothered Pork Chops in Onion Gravy

Serves 4

STARTERS

4	pork loin chops	1	large onion, sliced
1 tsp.	salt	2 Tblsp.	cooking oil
1 tsp.	pepper	1 cup	water
2 tsp.	McCormick's Season All	2 Tblsp.	cornstarch

46

GAMEPLAN

Place pork chops on one sheet of wax paper. Season with salt and pepper to taste. Heat oil in large skillet over medium heat. Add pork chops, cook until browned on both sides and cooked through, about 6 minutes turning once. Remove pork chops and transfer to platter. Drain half of the oil from the skillet. Add sliced onion to the same skillet used to cook pork chops. Cook onion over medium heat, until tender, about 2 to 3 minutes. Add water and pork chops and bring to a boil. Add cornstarch and stir to thicken.

OPTION PLAY

For thicker gravy add 1 tsp. of cornstarch and 1/2 cup of water.

69 Proved why reliable backup offensive linemen are so important in the NFL, by starting several games during 1995-96 campaign due to injuries along the line.

DERRICK DEESE
Barbecue Turkey

Serves 8–10

STARTERS

10 to 12 lb.	whole turkey
	salt and pepper

CITRUS MARINADE

1/3	cup orange juice
1/3 cup	chicken broth
1/4 cup	olive oil
2 to 3 cloves	garlic

GAMEPLAN

Remove lid from kettle-type barbecue; then open bottom dampers. Make a pile of 40–50 briquettes on fire grate; ignite. Let burn for 30–40 minutes until coals are covered by gray ash and some have a bright red glow. Arrange coals on each side of the barbecue and place a metal drip pan in the center. Set the cooking grill approximately 4–6 inches above the pan. 5–6 briquettes should be added to each side of the fire grate every 30–45 minutes to maintain an even temperature. Rinse turkey, pat dry. Sprinkle with salt and pepper. Truss wings. Place bird on grill above the drip pan. Cover kettle and adjust the dampers as needed to maintain an even heat. Brush with citrus marinade periodically throughout cooking time. Allow 15 minutes per pound. Turkey is done when meat near thighbone is no longer pink. Remove from barbecue, allow to stand 15-20 minutes before carving.

63 Latest in long line of standout linemen from Southern California, took three years to break into the 49ers' starting lineup—and has never looked back, Expected to hold down this position into the next decade as veteran line looks for changing of the guard.

RICKY ERVINS

Creole Chicken and Shrimp with Linguine

Serves 5

S T A R T E R S

4 Tblsp. · · · · · · · · · · **butter or margarine**

2 Tblsp. · · · · · · · · · · · · **vegetable oil**

1-1/4 to 1-1/2 lbs. · · · · · skinless, boneless **chicken breasts,** cut into 1/2 inch cubes

1 lb. · · · · · · · · · **shrimp,** peeled and deveined

1 tsp. · · · · · · · · · · · · · · **dried oregano**

1/2 tsp. each · · · · · · · · · · · **season salt, garlic powder, onion powder**

1/4 tsp. · · · · · · · · · · **pepper,** freshly ground

1/4 tsp. · · · · · · · · · · · · **cayenne pepper**

1 each onion, grn. bell pepper, chopped

4 cloves · · · · · · · · · · · · · · · **garlic** , crushed

1 · · · · · · · · · · · · · **tomato,** peeled and chopped

2 Tblsp. · · · · · · · · **Worcestershire sauce**

2 Tblsp. · · · · · · · · · · · · · · · **lemon juice**

1 lb. · · · · **linguine, cooked and drained**

S U B S T I T U T E S

· · · · · · · · · · · · · · · **rice or another pasta**

48

G A M E P L A N

In a large frying pan, melt 2 tablespoons of the butter and 1 tablespoon of oil over medium-high heat. Add chicken and shrimp. Sprinkle with oregano, season salt, pepper, garlic powder, onion powder and cayenne pepper. Sauté about 5 minutes, until chicken turns opaque and shrimp turns pink. Remove and set aside. Reduce heat to medium and add remaining 2 tablespoons of butter and 1 tablespoon of oil. Add onion and sauté until softened, about 3 minutes. Add green pepper and garlic and cook until pepper is crisp tender, 3 to 5 minutes. Add tomato, Worcestershire sauce, lemon juice. Return shrimp and chicken to pan, mix well, and simmer for 5 minutes, serve over linguine.

32 Was signed to add fire out of backfield, as he did with the Washington Redskins after being drafted out of Southern Cal. Another free-agent who couldn't beat them, so he joined them.

O P T I O N   P L A Y

This could be made healthier by cutting the oil and butter in half. Actually 2 tablespoons of oil could brown the ingredients. Add back 1/4 to 1/2 cup of the linguine liquid before serving so that dish is not dry.

ELVIS GRBAC
Homemade Tomato Sauce
[hand-off from wife Lori]
Serves 6

STARTERS

2 cans (16 oz.)	chopped tomatoes
1	medium onion
1 can (16 oz.)	crushed tomatoes
1 Tblsp.	fresh oregano, chopped
2 cloves	fresh garlic, chopped
1/4 cup	dry red wine
4 oz.	mushrooms, chopped
1	medium green pepper, chopped
1 tsp.	fresh basil, chopped
	black pepper, freshly ground
	dash red pepper, crushed salt

GAMEPLAN

Place chopped tomatoes, crushed tomatoes, red wine and garlic in large saucepan. Add onions and other vegetables, herbs, crushed red pepper, salt and pepper. Cook over medium heat, bring to a boil. Reduce heat and simmer at least 20 minutes until reduced and thickened. Serve over cooked pasta. Garnish with basil leaf. Add freshly grated parmesan cheese on top. The longer you cook the sauce, the better it will taste. Make sure to stir often.

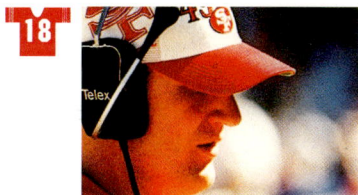

CARY CONKLIN
Veggie Chili

Serves 6

STARTERS

1/2 cup	bulgur wheat
2-1/2 cups	tomato juice
2 cups	kidney beans, cooked
2	small onions, chopped
1	green pepper, chopped
3 stalks	celery
3	carrots, chopped
2 cloves	garlic, minced
2	jalapenos, chopped
1 lb.	mushrooms, chopped
2 cups	water
3 Tblsp.	chili powder
2 tsp.	cumin
1 Tblsp.	tomato paste
	salt and pepper to taste

GAMEPLAN

Boil juice, strain over bulgur, set juice aside. In a Dutch oven (large pot) use oil to sauté veggies in this order: 1) onions, pepper, garlic—simmer for 5 minutes. 2) celery, carrots, jalapenos—simmer for 5 minutes. 3) mushrooms, tomato juice, water, tomato paste and seasonings—simmer for 15-20 minutes. 4) add beans—cook for 10 minutes. 5) add bulgur and cook for 15 minutes. Serve with warm bread.

18

6

TOMMY THOMPSON
Down Home Jambalaya

Serves 6

STARTERS

1-1/2 lbs.	**medium shrimp**
1 Tblsp.	**oil**
1	**medium onion,** chopped
2	**large cloves garlic,** minced
1-1/2 cups	**lean ham,** cubed
1 can (1 lb.)	**whole tomatoes,** chopped
2 bottles (8 oz.)	**clam juice**
1/3 cup	**parsley,** chopped
2 Tblsp.	**chili powder,** or to taste
3/4 tsp.	**dried thyme**
1 cup	**long grain rice**
	pepper to taste

50

GAMEPLAN

Clean shrimp. Set aside at room temperature. Heat oil in a large heavy pan with tight fitting lid. Add onion and garlic, cook until golden. Stir in ham, tomatoes and juice, clam juice, parsley, chili powder, thyme and pepper. Bring to a boil. Add rice, stir and cover. Cook over low heat (gently boiling) for 20 minutes. Stir in shrimp with a fork. Cook for 20-25 minutes longer.

DOUG BRIEN
Black Bean and Corn Tamale Pie

Serves 6

STARTERS

1	**medium onion,** chopped
3 cloves	**garlic,** chopped
1 Tblsp.	**oil**
2 cans (16 oz.)	**black beans,** drained
1 can (16 oz.)	**whole kernel corn,** drained
1 cup	**bottled taco sauce**
1 to 2 Tblsp.	**chili powder,** to taste
1 cup each	**Monterey Jack cheese and sharp cheddar,** shredded, combined

CORNMEAL CRUST

1-1/2 cups	**yellow cornmeal**
3-1/2 cups	**water**
1 tsp.	**salt**

GAMEPLAN

Prepare corn meal crust: In a large pan combine cornmeal, water and salt. Bring to a boil, stirring frequently. Cook 8 to 10 minutes until cornmeal mounds on spoon. Spread mixture over bottom and 1 inch up sides of a 3 to 3 1/2 quart shallow casserole. Set aside. Sauté onion and garlic in oil until soft. Add beans, corn, olives, taco sauce, chili powder and half the cheese. Spoon into cornmeal crust. Bake in middle of 350°F oven until hot, about 30 minutes. Sprinkle with remaining cheese, baking until cheese melts. To serve, combine lettuce, tomato and green onion, arrange over bubbly cheese.

J. J. STOKES
Red Cabbage and Apples

Serves 6

S T A R T E R S

1-1/2 lbs.	**red cabbage,** coarsely shredded
3	**tart cooking apples,** sliced
1/2 cup	**water**
1/4 cup	**sharp red wine vinegar**
1-1/2 tsp.	**salt**
1/3 cup	**brown sugar,** packed
big pinch	**all spice or cloves** powdered

G A M E P L A N

Coarsely shred cabbage, removing large ribs. Peel, core and slice apples. In a pot combine all ingredients except brown sugar. Mix well. Bring to a boil, cover, turn heat to medium-low. Simmer 20 minutes, stirring occasionally. Stir in brown sugar. Cook 5 to 10 minutes longer and serve.

A U D I B L E

Wonderful with knockwurst and mashed potatoes or roast pork and dumplings.

NATE SINGLETON
New Orleans Style Smothered Potatoes

Serves 4–6

S T A R T E R S

1	**large onion,** diced
1 clove	**garlic,** minced
6	**medium russet potatoes**
1 lb.	**lite smoked sausage**
1/2 tsp.	**garlic salt**
1/2 tsp.	**garlic powder**
1/2 tsp.	**Tony Chachere's Creole Seasoning**
1 tsp.	**season all**
1 tsp.	**parsley,** chopped
1 pinch	**cayenne pepper**
2 cups	**rice,** cooked

G A M E P L A N

Peel and thinly slice the potatoes to 1/4 inch thick. Cut up the sausage. Add all ingredients to a large skillet and cook over medium heat. Stir and mix well for about 5 minutes. Add enough water to cover the potatoes. Cook until potatoes are tender, stirring frequently. When potatoes are tender, turn on high heat for about 10 minutes to let water cook down. Serve over 2 cups of cooked rice.

51

83

88

MIKE CALDWELL
No Booze Ramos Fizz

Serves 8 (small servings)

S T A R T E R S

2 cups	ice, crushed
1 cup	Half & Half
1 cup	ginger ale
1/2 can (6 oz.)	frozen lemonade concentrate, thawed
1 Tblsp.	fresh lemon juice

G A M E P L A N

Fill jar of blender with 2 cups crushed ice. Add Half & Half, ginger ale, 1/2 can of thawed lemonade concentrate and lemon juice. Whisk until smooth. Great on a hot day!

81

CHRIS THOMAS
Winner Potato Salad

Serves 12

S T A R T E R S

3 lbs.	white potatoes, cooked, peeled and cubed
1/3 cup	canola oil
1/4 cup	cider vinegar
2 tsp.	salt
2 tsp.	dill weed
1/2 tsp.	pepper
1 cup	pimiento stuffed olives, sliced
1 cup	celery, thinly sliced
1/4 cup each	pimiento, ripe olives and red onion, chopped
3/4 cup	low-fat mayonnaise
1/4 cup	low-fat sour cream
2 Tblsp.	parsley, chopped

G A M E P L A N

Keep potatoes warm. Combine oil, vinegar, salt, dill weed and pepper. Mix well. Pour over potatoes, toss gently. Chill thoroughly. Add olives, celery, pimiento, ripe olives and onion. Combine mayonnaise, sour cream and parsley. Pour over salad mixture. Fold lightly until well combined.

89

52

BRETT CAROLAN
Skillet Cookie

Serves 6–8

S T A R T E R S

················· Pre-made cookie dough
···················· Vanilla Ice Cream
························ Chocolate Syrup

G A M E P L A N

Cut pre-made cookie dough into individual cookies or make one big cookie. Heat cookie dough in skillet until cooked. When done put one scoop of vanilla ice cream on top and smother with chocolate syrup.

A U D I B L E

The dessert of all desserts.

TED POPSON
Baked Salmon Steaks

Serves 4

S T A R T E R S

4 (6 oz.) ········ **salmon steaks or fillets,** 1-1/4 inch thick
1 Tblsp. each ····· **olive oil and melted butter**
1 large clove ············· **garlic,** pressed
1/4 tsp. ······· **tarragon leaves,** crumbled
3 Tblsp. each ················ **white wine and lemon juice**
2 Tblsp. ················· **parsley,** minced
salt and freshly cracked pepper to taste
4 ························ **lemon slices**

G A M E P L A N

Place salmon in a shallow oiled baking dish. Combine olive oil, melted butter, garlic, tarragon, white wine, lemon juice and parsley. Sprinkle salmon with salt and pepper. Spoon olive oil mixture over each piece of fish. Place a lemon slice on top of each. Bake at 450°F for 10–15 minutes, until desired doneness, spooning sauce over fish once.

A U D I B L E

Nice served on a bed of sautéed fresh spinach. Perfect with baked potato or rice on the side and salad.

53

ADAM WALKER
Sesame Chicken on a Stick

Serves 4

S T A R T E R S

8	**boneless, skinless chicken thighs or breasts,** cubed
2 Tblsp.	**sesame seeds,** toasted
1/3 cup	**chicken broth or white wine**
1/4 cup	**soy sauce**
1/4 cup	**canola oil**
1 Tblsp.	**lemon juice**
2 tsp.	**brown sugar,** packed
1/2 tsp.	**salt**
1/4 tsp.	**pepper**
1 large clove	**garlic,** pressed
2	**green onions,** minced

54

G A M E P L A N

Turn chicken into a glass or stainless steel container. Crush sesame seeds in a blender. Combine seeds with remaining ingredients. Mix well. Pour over chicken, refrigerate 1 hour or over night. Thread 4 or 5 pieces on small skewers. Broil 8 inches from moderate heat, basting and turning frequently until chicken is well browned and cooked through, about 25 minutes.

O P T I O N   P L A Y

By skinning the chicken, you will be eliminating much of its fat. Marinating the chicken will ensure its juiciness. Unlike fried chicken, you don't need to feel guilty eating Chicken on a Stick!

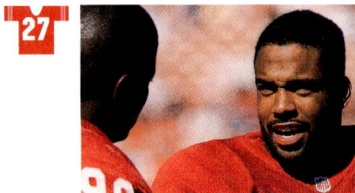

27

JAMAL WILLIS
Turkey Sausage Pizza

Serves 6–8

S T A R T E R S

1 (11")	**Italian bread shell** (like Boboli)
1 cup	**prepared spaghetti or pizza sauce**
3 cups	**mild cheddar or mozzarella cheese,** grated
3/4 lb.	**bulk turkey sausage**
2 cups	**mushrooms,** thinly sliced
1	**small onion,** thinly sliced
2 Tblsp.	**black olives**

G A M E P L A N

Preheat oven to 425°F. Place bread shell on baking sheet. Spread with prepared pizza sauce. Sprinkle with 1-1/2 cups cheese. In a skillet, sauté the onions, mushrooms and sausage until sausage is no longer pink and onions are soft. Spread on bread shell. Sprinkle with olives and remaining 1-1/2 cups cheese. Bake in hot oven for 10-15 minutes, until cheese is bubbly. Makes 1 pizza.

O P T I O N   P L A Y

You could probably reduce the cheese and not affect the taste.

24

TACKLE

FRANK POLLACK
Pasta Sauce with Meatballs
[recovery from wife Wendy]
Serves 8–12

S T A R T E R S

1	················· **medium onion,** chopped
1 can (28 oz.)	········ **crushed tomatoes**
1 can (28 oz.)	········ **pureed tomatoes**
1 can (15 oz.)	············ **tomato sauce**
2	············ **large cans of water**
1 lb.	················· **ground beef**
1/2 lb. each	········ **ground pork, veal**
1	·································· **egg**
3-4 pieces	············· **bread,** shredded
1-2 Tblsp.	······················· **sugar**
1-2 cloves	····················· **garlic**
1 can	··················· **tomato paste**
·· **salt, pepper, basil and oregano** to taste

G A M E P L A N

Begin by sautéing onion with garlic. Combine sautéed onion mix with crushed tomatoes, pureed tomatoes, tomato sauce, water and simmer over low heat. Combine ground beef, pork, veal, egg, bread, salt, pepper, basil and oregano. After mixing well roll into medium sized balls. Fry the meatballs in a skillet until browned, add tomato paste and the rest of the sauce. Simmer over low heat for approximately 10–12 minutes.

O P T I O N   P L A Y

Use ground turkey or lean ground beef instead of pork.

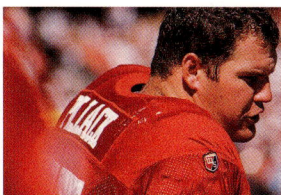

GUARD

TIM HANSHAW
Chicken Enchiladas
[recovered from wife Rachelle]
Serves 6

S T A R T E R S

4	···················· **chicken breasts**
2 cans	············· **Campbell's Cream**
	of Chicken Soup
1 pint	···················· **sour cream**
1 pkg.	················ **flour tortillas**
1	··································· **tomato**
1 can	································ **olives**
1/2 each	···· **green pepper, red pepper**
1/4-1/3 cup	······· **mozzarella cheese**
1/4-1/3 cup	·········· **cheddar cheese**
····················· **mushrooms, onion**

G A M E P L A N

Boil chicken breasts and then shred. Mix 2 cans of chicken soup with 1 pint of sour cream. Chop tomato, mushrooms, onion, olives and peppers. Grate the cheese. Portion out the chicken, sauce, cheese, tomato, mushrooms, onion, olive and peppers equally into the 12 tortilla shells. Put all 12 tortillas in a big baking dish and pour remaining sauce on top. Sprinkle with cheese. Bake at 350°F until the cheese bubbles, about 20-30 minutes.

O P T I O N   P L A Y

Use the low-sodium soup for lower salt intake and the light sour cream for less fat and calories.

DEFENSE

57 One of a handful of veterans who signed with the 49ers for their Super Bowl XXIX run. Former New Orleans Saint always played his best against the 49ers; now he lends outside pass rush and on-field savvy.

RICKEY JACKSON

Apple Cranberry Crumble

Serves 6–8

STARTERS

5 · · · · · · · · · · · **medium baking apples,** peeled, thinly sliced

1/2 cup · · · · · · · · · · · · **dried cranberries**

1/4 cup · · · · · · · · · · · · · · · **orange juice**

2/3 cup · · · · · · · · · · **brown sugar,** packed

1/2 cup · **flour**

1/2 cup · **oatmeal**

1/2 tsp. each · cinnamon and nutmeg

1 Tblsp. · · · · · · · · · · · · **orange peel,** grated

1/3 cup · · · · · · · · · · · · · **walnuts,** chopped

1/4 cup · · · · · · · · · · · · · · · · · · · **canola oil**

· · · · · · · · · · · · · · · · · **nonfat vanilla yogurt**

GAMEPLAN

Combine apples, cranberries and orange juice. Turn into lightly oiled 8 inch square pan or 9 inch round pie plate. Blend all remaining ingredients well. Spoon over apple mixture. Bake in middle of oven at 375°F for 30 minutes, until apples are tender and topping is nicely browned. Serve with yogurt.

59

97 The 49ers traded up for this Notre Dame standout in the first round of the 1994 draft—and received immediate return. Young teams with Dana Stubblefield to provide huge inside push.

BRYANT YOUNG
Southwest Veggie Sauté

Serves 6–8

S T A R T E R S

1 · · · · · **large onion,** halved and thinly sliced

1 · · · · · **large red pepper,** cut into thin strips

3 cloves · · · · · · · · · · · · · · · · **garlic,** minced

1 · · · · · · · · · · · · · **jalapeno chili,** minced

2 Tblsp. · · · · · · · · · · · · · · · **olive oil** (or less)

3 · · · · · · · · · · **zucchini,** cut into 1/4 inch slices

1-1/2 cups · · · · · · · · · · **corn,** fresh or canned

1 tsp. · **sugar**

· · · · · · · · · · · · · · · **salt and pepper** to taste

1/4 cup · · · · · · · · · · · · · · **cilantro,** minced

1/2 cup · · · · · · · **Monterey Jack cheese**
(optional), shredded

G A M E P L A N

In a large skillet sauté onion, red pepper, garlic and chili in olive oil over medium high heat for 5 minutes, stirring. Add zucchini, corn and sugar. Salt and pepper to taste. Reduce heat and sauté 5 to 8 minutes longer until zucchini is just cooked. Stir in cilantro and cheese, if desired.

61

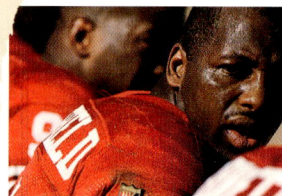

94 Named 1993 Defensive Rookie of the Year as a top pick from Kansas, then was named to the Pro Bowl during his sophomore campaign in 1994. Considered a Michael Carter of the 90s. Built like a defensive tackle.

DANA STUBBLEFIELD

Shrimp Dip on the Bay

Serves 4–6

STARTERS

3 oz.	**cream cheese**
2 Tblsp.	**mayonnaise**
1 Tblsp.	**ketchup**
1 tsp.	**mustard**
big pinch	**garlic powder**
1/4 cup	**celery,** finely minced

1 tsp.	**onion** minced
1 cup	**bay shrimp,** chopped
	parsley, chopped
	celery, cut into sticks
	chips
	bread sticks

GAMEPLAN

Combine cream cheese, mayonnaise, mustard, ketchup, garlic powder, celery and onion in a bowl. Beat until smooth. Fold in shrimp and chopped parsley. Dip with celery sticks on chips or bread sticks. Serve at room temperature.

63

96 Known for amazing speed as a big man—before he lost over 60 pounds. Retained his strength and speed to give team much-needed pressure from the outside. Drafted in 1990 out of Washington.

DENNIS BROWN

DB's Favorite Stuffed Peppers
[hand-off from wife Danielle]
Serves 4

STARTERS

4	large green peppers
1-1/2 lbs.	ground sirloin
1/3 cup	onion, chopped
1/2 cup	water
1 cup	ketchup
1-1/2 cups	long grain rice, cooked
1/2 tsp.	dried basil
1/2 cup	cheddar cheese, shredded
	salt, pepper and garlic to taste

SUBSTITUTES

1-1/2 lbs.	ground turkey
1/4 cup	cheddar cheese

GAMEPLAN

Remove stem ends, membranes and seeds from peppers. Immerse peppers in boiling water for 3 minutes. Sprinkle insides with salt and invert on paper towels to drain well. In a skillet cook meat, salt, pepper, garlic and onion until the meat is brown and onion is tender. Drain the fat. Add 1/2 cup water, stir in ketchup, rice and basil. Simmer for 10 minutes. Fill peppers with meat mixture. Place in an 8 x 8 x 2 inch baking dish. Sprinkle with cheese. Bake at 375°F for 15 minutes.

OPTION PLAY

For low-fat recipe use ground turkey instead of sirloin. Use 1/4 cup of cheddar cheese on top.

54 How many rookies start their first season, culminating with a Super Bowl? How many return as a standout blitzing linebacker their second season? How many do this as a sixth-round draft pick from West Chester?

LEE WOODALL

Mom's Ham and Beans

Serves 6–8

S T A R T E R S

4 lbs.	smoked picnic ham (lean as possible)	2	medium onions, quartered
3	bay leaves	1-1/2 lbs.	green beans (Kentucky wonders or Italian flat beans)
1 tsp. each	whole cloves and pepper		ham broth
6 to 8	white potatoes, halved		vinegar

G A M E P L A N

Place ham, bay leaves, cloves and pepper in heavy pot. Cover two-thirds of ham with water. Bring to a boil, reduce heat, cover and simmer for about 2 hours until ham is tender. This may be done early in the day. When ready to serve, place ham in low oven to keep warm. Cook potatoes and onions in broth until done, adding green beans the last 5-8 minutes of cooking. Spoon vegetables from broth. Arrange platter with ham.

O P T I O N   P L A Y

Try cooking the ham early in the day and chill the cooking broth. You can then skim the hardened fat off the top of the ham stock, before cooking the vegetables. You'll have all the ham flavor, without any of the ham fat.

67

50 Cal grad played several years in San Diego before joining the 49ers last season for their Super Bowl run. Known as a plugger inside, stuffing the run while serving as team leader in locker room.

GARY PLUMMER

Grilled Salmon with Chopped Tomatoes

Serves 2

STARTERS

2 ···················· **salmon fillets**

···················· **fresh lemon**

6 ············· **Roma tomatoes,** chopped

3 cloves ················ **garlic,** crushed

···················· **basil, fresh or dry**

2 Tblsp. ···················· **olive oil**

···················· **salt and pepper** to taste

69

GAMEPLAN

Grill salmon on barbecue or broil in oven, squeeze lemon. Chop up tomatoes, crush garlic. Combine all ingredients in a bowl and add oil. Salt and pepper to taste. In a skillet cook tomato mixture on high heat for a couple minutes. Place salmon on a plate and pour mixture on top of salmon. Serve with fresh steamed vegetables and wild rice.

OPTION PLAY

You can also use swordfish.

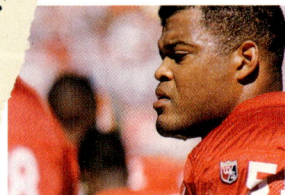

51 Son of former heavy-weight champ became first player in NFL history to play on three consecutive Super Bowl champions after leaving Dallas for San Francisco last season. Known for run defense.

KEN NORTON JR.

All-American Potato Salad

Serves 4

STARTERS

1/2 cup	**bulgar wheat**
3/4 cup	**hot water**
1/2 lb.	**small red potatoes,** cooked and halved
2 cups	**mushrooms,** sliced
1	**medium tomato,** seeded and chopped
1/2 cup each	**parsley and mint,** chopped
1/2 cup	**small pitted ripe olives**
1/3 cup	**red onion,** minced
	garden lettuce
	tomato, chopped (optional)

LEMON DRESSING

1/3 cup	**canola oil**
1/4 cup	**fresh lemon juice**
1 tsp.	**salt**
1/4 tsp.	**pepper**

GAMEPLAN

Combine bulgar and water in 2 quart bowl. Let stand 15 minutes. Prepare lemon dressing. (LEMON DRESSING: Combine oil, lemon juice, salt and pepper. Mix well.) If potatoes are larger, cut into quarters or eighths. Squeeze bulgar dry if all the water is absorbed.

Combine bulgar, potatoes, and mushrooms with the dressing. Toss well. Add all remaining ingredients except lettuce and chopped tomato. Mix well. Let marinate 1 hour, stirring occasionally.

71

25 When he arrived in 1989 out of Jacksonville State, people said he looked like a young Ronnie Lott. Now he acts Lott's former role as veteran cornerback in young secondary. And proud to be a disciple.

ERIC DAVIS

Stuffed French Bread

Serves 4

STARTERS

1 stick ·················· **butter,** softened

1/2 cup ······· **mayonnaise** (non-fat okay)

1/2 cup ······ **parmesan cheese,** grated

2 ············ **large garlic cloves,** pressed

1 tsp. each ···· **Worcestershire sauce and paprika**

6 ············· **green onions,** thinly sliced

1 ·············· **French bread,** long loaf

GAMEPLAN

Beat together butter, mayonnaise and cheese until well mixed. Add garlic, Worcestershire sauce, paprika and green onions. Fold together with spatula. Slice bread in 3/4 inch slices, but not through the bottom crust. Spread slices with the cheese mixture—be generous. Wrap bread in aluminum foil. Bake in 350°F oven about 15–20 minutes, until piping hot.

AUDIBLE

Good with barbecue chicken or rice and vegetables.

73

23 Used to level 49ers with his monster hits—so 49ers signed him away from the Rams and converted him from strong safety to cornerback. No. 33 player selected overall by San Diego out of Fresno State in 1992.

MARQUEZ POPE
Monday Night Tacos

Serves 4

STARTERS

4 · **corn tortillas**

1 pound · · **ground turkey or lean beef**

1 Tblsp. · **oil**

1 · · · · · · · · · · · · · **medium onion,** chopped

1 can · · · · · · · · · · · · · · · **chili with beans**

1/2 cup each · · · · **carrot and zucchini,** grated

2 cups · · · · · · · **romaine lettuce,** shredded

1-1/3 cups · · · **Monterey Jack cheese,** shredded

1-1/3 cups · **salsa** (homemade or purchased)

big pinch · · · · · · · · · · · **cayenne pepper**

· · · · · · · · · · · **salt, oregano, cumin** to taste

· **sour cream**

· **avocado slices**

· **radish slices**

· · · · · · · · · · · · · · **chopped green onion**

GAMEPLAN

Bake tortillas in 350°F oven for 8 minutes, until crisp. Set aside. In a large skillet brown turkey or beef in oil over medium heat, stirring to break up. Add onion and cook 5 minutes longer. Add chili powder, oregano, cumin and salt to taste. Combine well. Cover and simmer for 10 minutes. To serve, place a tortilla on plate. Top with one-fourth turkey bean mixture. Top with one-fourth of remaining ingredients in order given. Repeat for 3 more tacos.

75

46 Perennial All-Pro left Arizona Cardinals to play in his first Super Bowl. Plays best when allowed to create havoc at line of scrimmage. Part of best safety combo in the league.

TIM McDONALD
Mexican Steak Tartare

Serves 8–10

STARTERS

1 lb.	**filet mignon**	1/2 tsp.	**coarse black pepper**
3 to 4 Tblsp.	**fresh lime juice**		**lettuce leaves**
1 or 2	**jalapeno chilis,** finely minced		**crisp corn tortilla triangles**
1/2 cup	**red onion,** minced		**cilantro,** chopped
1/4 cup	**cilantro,** chopped		**red pepper,** cut in slivers
3/4 tsp.	**salt**		

GAMEPLAN

Finely mince or grind meat. Keep very cold. Combine meat, lime juice, jalapeno chili, onion, cilantro, salt and pepper. Mix well, using 2 spoons or forks. Arrange lettuce on serving plate. Mound steak tartare in middle. Surround with tortilla triangles. Garnish with cilantro and red pepper.

77

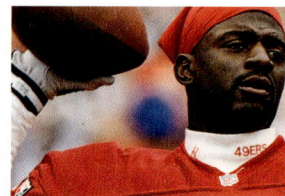

36 Moved to safety full-time as 49ers made their run for a fifth Super Bowl title. Played mostly cornerback after joining the 49ers as fifth round pick from Iowa in 1990. Now considered one of best safeties in league.

MERTON HANKS

Barbecue Kebobs

Serves 4

STARTERS

2-1/2 to 3 lbs. ········ **top sirloin beef**
(1-1/2 inches thick)

8 ···· **Roma tomatoes,** halved (not too ripe)

1 ················ **large yellow pepper,**
seeded and cut into 1-1/2 inch chunks

1 ················ **large green pepper,**
seeded and cut into 1-1/2 chunks

MARINADE

1 cup ················· **burgundy wine**

1/4 cup ······················· **olive oil**

2 large cloves ··········· **garlic,** pressed

1/2 tsp. each ·············· **thyme and
dried rosemary,** crushed

GAMEPLAN

Prepare marinade by combining wine, olive oil, garlic, thyme and rosemary. Cut beef into 1-1/2 inch cubes. Add beef to marinade. Cover, refrigerate 6 hours or overnight, stirring occasionally. Remove meat from marinade. Reserve marinade. On eight metal skewers thread meat alternately with vegetables. Grill 6 inches above medium coals. Baste with marinade. Turn until all sides are browned. Test meat for desired doneness.

79

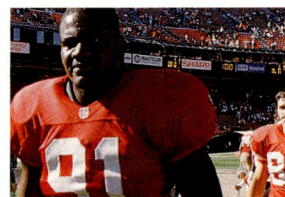

91 Former top pick out of Colorado went from worst team (Cincinnati) to best team (49ers) in 1995. Bengals thought they could re-sign him; 49ers snagged another veteran to apply pressure on quarterbacks.

ALFRED WILLIAMS
Tailgate Chicken

Serves 4–6

S T A R T E R S

1 (3-1/2 lb.) ······· **frying chicken,** cut up

2 Tblsp. each ··· **butter and canola oil**

2 Tblsp. ·················· **lemon juice**

1/3 cup ·········· **fresh bread crumbs**

1/3 cup ········· **toasted wheat germ**

1/3 cup ····· **parmesan cheese,** grated

3/4 tsp. ····························· **salt**

81

G A M E P L A N

Wash and dry chicken pieces. Melt butter and add lemon juice. Combine bread crumbs, wheat germ, cheese and salt. Brush chicken pieces with lemon butter. Roll in crumb mixture. Arrange skin side up on an oiled baking pan. Bake 375°F for 45 minutes until juices run clear.

TYRONNE DRAKEFORD

Easy Lasagna

Serves 8

S T A R T E R S

10	lasagna noodles (10 x 2 inches)
1 cup	ricotta cheese
1/2 pound	Italian sausage, browned and drained
3 cups	mushrooms, thinly sliced
2 cups	zucchini, shredded
1 cup	Monterey Jack cheese (4 oz.), shredded
1 cup	parmesan cheese, grated
	parsley, chopped

Z E S T Y   S A U C E

1 jar	meatless spaghetti sauce
1-1/4 cup	red wine
2 Tblsp.	oregano
2 tsp.	garlic powder
8 cups	spinach leaves

82

G A M E P L A N

Prepare zesty sauce: In large saucepan combine spaghetti sauce, 1-1/4 cup red wine, oregano, garlic powder and spinach. Bring to a boil, reduce heat and simmer uncovered for 10 minutes. Spread uncooked noodles with ricotta cheese. Spoon about 2 cups sauce over bottom of 13 x 9 x 2 baking dish. Arrange 5 noodles over sauce, overlapping slightly and staggering end to end. Spoon another 2 cups sauce over noodles. Arrange mushrooms, zucchini, and sausage over sauce. Repeat with remaining noodles and sauce. Sprinkle Monterey Jack cheese over top. Cover tightly with heavy-duty or double thickness foil forming a dome. Bake in middle of oven at 375°F. Uncover. Sprinkle with parmesan cheese and chopped parsley.

22 Latest in long line of young defensive back "finds" drafted by the 49ers. Was second-round pick in 1994 out of Virginia Tech and is inching closer to starting lineup with each contest.

DEDRICK DODGE
Half-Time Punch

Makes 5 quarts

STARTERS

1 can (12 oz.) · · · · · · **frozen orange juice concentrate,** thawed

2 quarts · · · · · · · · **grapefruit soda,** chilled

1 quart each · · · · · · · · · **ginger ale and club soda,** chilled

1 block (5 inch x 5 inch) **(or ring)** · · · · · · **ice**

· **orange slices**

· **grapefruit wedges**

· **mint sprigs**

83

GAMEPLAN

Combine orange juice concentrate, grapefruit soda, ginger ale and club soda in 6 quart punch bowl. Add ice, garnish with orange, grapefruit and mint.

33 Joined 49ers in 1994 and provided depth in secondary and strength on special teams. First signed by Seattle in 1990 out of Florida State.

TIM HARRIS

Yogurt Fruit Smoothie

Serves 2

STARTERS

2 · · · · · · · · · · · · · · · **bananas,** peeled and sliced

2 cups · · · · · **strawberries,** fresh or frozen

1 cup · · · · · · · · · · · · · · · · · · **orange juice**

1 cup · · · · · · · · · · · · · · · · · · · **plain yogurt**

pinch · · · · · · · · · · · · **nutmeg or cinnamon**

GAMEPLAN

Put all ingredients in blender jar. Blend until smooth.
Pour into two tall glasses and enjoy.

99 First joined the team via trade from Green Bay in 1993, then left for Philadelphia the next season only to return to the 49ers as a major factor in their Super Bowl XXIX title run. Considered one of the best outside pass rushers in the game.

ANTONIO GOSS

Down Home Spaghetti and Meatballs

Serves 4–6

STARTERS

1/2 cup	**onion,** minced
1/3 cup	**celery,** minced
2 cloves	**garlic,** minced
1 Tblsp.	**olive oil**
1 Tblsp.	**dried basil,** crumbled
1-1/2 tsp.	**dried oregano,** crumbled
1/4 tsp.	**dried rosemary,** crumbled
1 tsp.	**sugar**
	salt to taste
1 can (28 oz.)	Italian plum **tomatoes,** chopped

1 Tblsp.	**cider vinegar**
2 cups	**mushrooms,** sliced
	spaghetti, cooked
1/2 cup	**parmesan cheese**
2 Tblsp.	**parsley,** chopped
1 lb.	**ground beef**
1/2 cup	**red wine or water**
1/4 tsp. each	**black pepper, nutmeg**
1	**egg**

SUBSTITUTES

chili pepper flakes, crushed

GAMEPLAN

Prepare meatballs: Combine 1 pound beef, 1 egg, and 1/2 cup red wine or water. Add 1 cup soft bread crumbs, 1/2 cup grated parmesan cheese, 1 large garlic clove, 2 tablespoons chopped parsley, 3/4 teaspoon salt, 1/4 teaspoon each black pepper and nutmeg. Mix well. Make 24 meatballs. Bake on a lightly oiled pan 375°F for 15 minutes, until browned. Keep warm

98 The only member of the 49ers' Super Bowl XXIV defense to also play in Super Bowl XXIX. Known for his pivotal role on special teams.

For sauce: Sauté onion, celery, and garlic in oil until soft. Add herbs, sugar, salt, tomatoes, vinegar and chili pepper flakes, if desired. Bring to a boil, reduce heat and simmer 15 minutes. Put cooked spaghetti on serving platter. Spoon over sauce. Top with meatballs. Sprinkle with parmesan cheese and chopped parsley.

MICHAEL BRANDON
Stir-Fry Pizza

Serves 6–8

STARTERS

1	(11") **Italian bread shell** (like Boboli)
2	**medium-size ripe tomatoes,** thinly sliced
2 cups	**mozzarella cheese,** grated
1/3 cup	**parmesan cheese,** grated
2 Tblsp.	**olive oil**
2 cloves	**garlic,** pressed
1	**medium onion,** thinly sliced
2 cups	**broccoli florets**
2 cup	**mushrooms,** sliced
1-1/2 cups	**zucchini,** thinly sliced
1/2 cup	**each yellow and red pepper** slivered
1/2 Tblsp.	**salt**
1 Tblsp.	**cracked black pepper**

GAMEPLAN

Preheat oven to 425°F. Place bread shell on baking sheet. Arrange tomato slices over shell, covering completely. Sprinkle with cheeses. Bake in hot oven 10–15 minutes, until cheese is bubbly. Meanwhile, in a large skillet, heat olive oil. Sauté garlic and onion in oil for five minutes. Add broccoli and sauté five minutes longer. Add remaining vegetables and sauté until all are tender-crisp. Sprinkle with salt and pepper. Remove hot pizza-bread from oven. Top with stir-fry vegetables and serve immediately.

JAMAL FOUNTAINE
Sunday Pot Roast Supper

Serves 6–8

STARTERS

3 to 4 lbs.	**chuck roast,** 2 inches thick
1	**medium large onion,** finely grated
3 large cloves	**garlic,** pressed
3 Tblsp.	**paprika**
1 Tblsp.	**chili powder**
1-1/2 tsp.	**salt**
1 large	**onion,** cut into 1/2 inch slices
3/4 cup	**beef broth or water**
	vegetables
	parsley, chopped

GAMEPLAN

Place meat in small heavy roasting pan. Combine grated onion, garlic, paprika, chili powder and salt to form a paste. Spread one half of paste on top of meat. Bake at 500°F for 15 minutes. Turn roast. Spread remaining paste over. Bake 15 minutes longer. Arrange onion slices over top. Cover tightly, using foil under lid, if necessary. Bake 325°F for 2 hours. Add potatoes, carrots, parsnips and/or other vegetables. Cover, bake 1 hour longer. Serve pot roast on platter surrounded with vegetables.

88

DARRYL HALL
Low-Fat Enchiladas

Serves 4

S T A R T E R S

1 lb. · · · · · · · · · · · · **ground turkey breast**
1 envelope · · · · · · · **taco seasoning mix**
low-fat cheddar cheese, grated (as needed)
1 · **red onion**
2 large cans · · · · · · · · · · **enchilada sauce**
1 pkg. · · · · · · · · · · · · · · · · · · **corn tortillas**

G A M E P L A N

Preheat oven to 350°F. Use large baking dish. Grate cheddar cheese in a large bowl, set aside. Chop the onion into fine pieces, set aside. Prepare ground turkey as on the taco seasoning envelope. Warm enchilada sauce in saucepan over low heat. Warm two tortillas at a time in microwave (30 seconds with paper towel over them). Dip the tortillas in the sauce. Fill with meat, onion, cheese and roll them in large baking dish. When the dish is full, pour the remaining sauce over the top. Cover with more cheese and bake in oven 350°F for about 20 minutes or until cheese is melted and the mixture is bubbling.

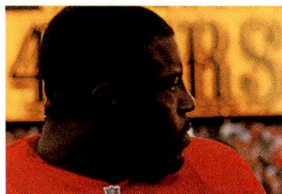

MICHAEL WILLIAMS
Hash with Eggs

Serves 4

S T A R T E R S

1 · · · · · · · · · · · · · · · · · **large onion,** chopped
1 · · · · · · · · · · · · · · · · **green pepper,** minced
1 Tblsp. · **oil**
2 cans · · · · · · · · · · **Mary's Kitchen** (15 oz.)
· · · · · · · · · · · · · · · · · · · **corned beef hash**
1 cup · · · · · · · · · · · **cheddar cheese,** cubed
4 · **large eggs**
2 Tblsp. · · · · · · **parmesan cheese,** grated
· · · · · · · · · · · · · · · · **salt and pepper** to taste

G A M E P L A N

Sauté onion and green pepper in oil until soft in a large skillet. Add corned beef hash. Continue to brown, using metal spatula to stir. Remove from heat. Fold in the cheese. Spoon into lightly oiled 8 inch baking dish. Break eggs on top. Sprinkle with salt, pepper and cheese. Bake 350°F until eggs are set.

O P T I O N   P L A Y

Can be prepared on grill in iron skillet. Good for breakfast, lunch or dinner.

COACHES

BILL McPHERSON
Zucchini Bread

Makes 3 loaves

S T A R T E R S

3	eggs
1 cup	oil
1 tsp.	vanilla
2 cups	sugar
2 cups	zucchini, grated
3 cups	flour
1 tsp.	baking powder
2 tsp.	baking soda
1 tsp.	salt
2 tsp.	cinammon
1/2 cup	walnuts, chopped

G A M E P L A N

Beat eggs until foamy, add oil, vanilla, sugar and zucchini. Blend together. Add all dry ingredients, walnuts last. Pour into greased bread pans and bake 1 hour at 325°F.

JERRY ATTAWAY
Gourmet Spinach Salad

Serves 8

S T A R T E R S

2 bunches	fresh spinach (about 2 pounds)
1/4 to 1/2 lb.	lean bacon, cooked and crumbled
1/2 cup	green onion, thinly sliced
2	red apples, cored and cut into chunks
1	hard cooked egg, grated
1/4 cup	dry roasted peanuts

M U S T A R D   D R E S S I N G

2 Tblsp.	mayonnaise
2 Tblsp.	Dijon-style mustard
2 Tblsp.	red wine vinegar
1/4 tsp. each	salt, sugar, and coarse black pepper
1/2 cup	olive oil

G A M E P L A N

Prepare Mustard Dressing: Whisk together mayonnaise, Dijon-style mustard, red wine vinegar, salt, sugar, pepper and olive oil until smooth. Set aside. Wash, dry, de-stem and crisp spinach. When ready to serve combine salad ingredients in a bowl. Toss with dressing.

MARC TRESTMAN
Salmon Spread

Serves 4–6

STARTERS

1 can (1 lb.) ················· **red salmon,** drain and remove bones
1 pkg. (8 oz.) ·············· **cream cheese**
1 Tblsp. ···················· **lemon juice**
1 Tblsp. ······ **onion,** grated and sponged dry
1 tsp. ····················· **horseradish**
1/4 tsp. ························ **salt**
1/2 tsp. ···················· **liquid smoke**
3 Tblsp. ·············· **parsley,** chopped
···· **crackers, melba toast or baguette**

GAMEPLAN

Using a wooden spoon or electric mixer combine all ingredients except crackers, until well blended. Pack into a serving bowl and surround with crackers. Serve at room temperature.

PETE CARROLL
Barbecue Chicken
[**pictured on front cover**]
Serves 4

STARTERS

2 ··· **broiler chickens** (2 1/2 lbs. each), split
················· **salt and pepper** to taste
1 cup ················ **red jalapeno jelly**
1/4 cup ·········· **Dijon style mustard**
2 Tblsp. ···························· **oil**
2 Tblsp. ······················ **ketchup**

93

GAMEPLAN

Rinse chicken and pat dry. With skin side up press firmly to crack bones slightly. Salt and pepper both sides. In a small saucepan combine jelly, mustard, oil and ketchup. Heat until jelly is melted. Keep warm. Grill chicken 6 inches above medium coals. Turn several times. Baste frequently as the chicken cooks.

DWAINE "PEE WEE" BOARD
Pee Wee's Coleslaw

Serves 6

STARTERS

6 cups	cabbage (about 1 head), finely julienned
1 cup	carrots, grated (use hand grater)
1/2 cup	red cabbage, finely julienned
1/2 cup	red onion, finely chopped

DRESSING

3 cups	cider vinegar
1 cup	mayonnaise
1 cup	sugar
1 tsp.	celery salt
1 Tblsp.	celery seeds
	salt and white pepper to taste

GAMEPLAN

Toss first 4 ingredients together in a large salad bowl. Dressing: Bring vinegar to a boil and add the sugar. Bring to a boil again stirring occasionally. Cool. After completely cool, add mayonnaise, salt, pepper, celery salt and celery seeds. Blend well and toss with cabbage mixture.

OPTION PLAY

You might try to cut back on the sugar a bit.

TOM HOLMOE
Chocolate Fondue

Makes 1-1/4 cups

STARTERS

4 oz.	semi-sweet chocolate
4 Tblsp.	butter
1/3 cup	whipping cream
1/2 cup	powdered sugar, sifted
1 tsp.	vanilla
	strawberries
	pear slices
	dried apricots
	biscotti

GAMEPLAN

In a small heavy saucepan melt chocolate and butter. Whisk in cream, powdered sugar and vanilla, stirring until smooth. To serve put in a small candle warmed fondue pot. Surround with strawberries, pear slices, dried apricots and biscotti.

94

NEAL DAHLEN

Perfect Picnic Brisket with Potato Salad

Serves 4–6

STARTERS

1 lb.	brisket of beef cooked	MUSTARD DRESSING	
	butter lettuce leaves	1 can (2 oz.)	anchovy fillets, drained
4 cups	potatoes (1-1/2 lbs.), cooked and sliced	2/3 cup	olive oil (not extra virgin)
1	small red onion, thinly sliced	1/2 cup	sharp red wine vinegar
1/3 cup	parsley, chopped	2 tsp.	Dijon mustard
3	sour pickles, sliced lengthwise	2 tsp.	salt
		1/4 tsp.	pepper

GAMEPLAN

Prepare mustard dressing: Drain anchovies, chop enough anchovies to measure one tablespoon. Mix together olive oil, red wine vinegar, mustard, salt and pepper. Slice warm brisket in 1/4 inch sections. Line a medium sized platter with lettuce leaves. Arrange brisket slices so that they overlap down the middle of platter. Drizzle with 1/3 cup dressing. Toss potatoes, onion and parsley with remaining dressing. Place or spoon potato salad on either side of meat. Tuck in pickle spears. Garnish salad with remaining anchovies and chopped parsley.

CARL JACKSON

Baked Eggplant Rolls

Serves 4

STARTERS

1	eggplant	1/2 cup	low-fat mozzarella cheese shredded
2 cups	light marinara sauce		
1 cup	Ricotta Pesto		

GAMEPLAN

Cut the eggplant lengthwise into 1/4 inch slices. Arrange the sliced eggplant in a single layer on a non-stick baking sheet. Bake in oven inches from heat until softened (3-5 minutes). Spread 1/4 cup of sauce on bottom of baking dish. Place equal amounts of pesto in center of each eggplant slice. Fold inside of eggplant over pesto to form a small package. Arrange rolls seam-side down in baking dish. Top with remaining 1-1/2 cups sauce and sprinkle with mozzarella. Bake at 375°F until eggplant is tender, about 40 minutes. This recipe goes well with a light pasta and chicken breast.

LARRY KIRKSEY

Cornbread Stuffing Casserole

Serves 12

STARTERS

1 pkg. (13 oz.)	cornbread mix	2 tsp.	salt
2 cups each	onion and celery, chopped	1/2 tsp.	pepper
2	medium green peppers, cored and coarsely chopped	1 can (1 lb.)	whole corn, drained
2 Tblsp.	butter	3/4 cup	pecans or walnuts, chopped
2 Tblsp.	canola oil	1/2 cup	parsley, minced
3 cups	mushrooms, sliced	1	large egg, beaten
1 Tblsp. each	dried sage and thyme, crumbled	1 cup	chicken broth

GAMEPLAN

Prepare cornbread using package instructions. Set aside. Using a large skillet, sauté onion, celery and green pepper in butter and oil until tender-crisp. Add mushrooms, sage, thyme, salt, pepper and corn. Cook 10 minutes longer, stirring occasionally. Mix cold vegetables in a large bowl. Fold in pecans, parsley, egg and crumbled corn bread. Add enough chicken broth to moisten. Turn into an oiled 3 quart baking dish. Bake covered at 375°F for 40 minutes or until heated through. Uncover and bake 10 minutes longer.

GREG KNAPP

Ambrosia

Serves 6–8

STARTERS

3 cans (11 oz.)	mandarin orange segments	3/4 cup	angel flake coconut
1 can (20 oz.)	pineapple chunks in juice	1 cup	sour cream
1 cup	miniature marshmallows	2 Tblsp.	light brown sugar, packed

GAMEPLAN

Thoroughly drain mandarin oranges and pineapple. Combine fruits with marshmallows and coconut. Stir together sour cream and brown sugar until well blended. Gently fold fruit mixture into sour cream mixture. Chill at least 2-3 hours to blend flavors.

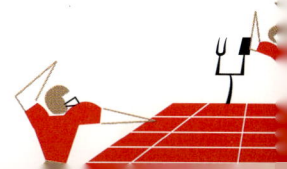

ALAN LOWRY

Baked Beans

Serves 12

STARTERS

1/2 lb.	lean bacon, cut into 1-inch strips
3 cans (28 ounces)	baked beans
1-1/2 cup	onions, finely chopped
1/3 cup	brown sugar, packed
1/3 cup	maple syrup
3 Tblsp.	prepared horseradish
2 tsp.	dry mustard
1 tsp.	salt
1/2 tsp.	black pepper
2 Tblsp.	cider vinegar

GAMEPLAN

Cook bacon until almost crisp. Drain and reserve 2 tablespoons of drippings. In a large bowl combine bacon, drippings and all remaining ingredients. Mix well. Turn into a bean pot or casserole. Bake, tightly covered at 300°F for 1-1/2 hours. Uncover and bake 30 minutes longer.

BOBB McKITTRICK

Deviled Eggs

Serves 12

STARTERS

6	large eggs, hard-cooked
1/2 cup	small curd non-fat cottage cheese
2 Tblsp.	mustard
2 Tblsp.	sweet pickle, minced
1/4 tsp. each	salt and paprika
2-3 Tblsp.	mayonnaise
	pimiento pieces
	parsley

GAMEPLAN

Cut shelled eggs in half, length-wise. Remove yolks, set aside whites. Mash yolks with back of fork. Beat in cottage cheese and mustard until smooth. Mix in chopped parsley, pickle, salt, paprika and as much mayonnaise as needed for a soft mounding consistency. Spoon filling into egg whites. Garnish with pimiento and parsley.

JOHN MARSHALL

Lazy Day Minestrone

Serves 4–6

STARTERS

1/4 lb.	Italian sausage, remove from casing
2 Tblsp.	olive oil
1	large onion, chopped
2 cloves	garlic, chopped
2-1/2 cups	water
2 cans	beef or chicken broth
1 can (1 lb.)	Italian tomatoes, chopped, reserving juice
1 can (1 lb.)	white or red beans, drained
1 cup each	carrot, mushrooms and zucchini, thinly sliced
1	bay leaf, crumbled
1-1/2 to 2 tsp. each	basil and oregano, crumbled
1 tsp.	salt
	pepper to taste
1/2 cup	fettucine or spaghetti, broken
	parmesan cheese, grated

GAMEPLAN

In a large pot, brown sausage in olive oil. Stir in onions and garlic, sauté 5 minutes longer. Add all remaining ingredients except parmesan cheese. Bring to a boil; reduce heat, simmering for 15 minutes until pasta is done. Taste for salt and pepper. Serve with parmesan cheese.

BO PELINI

Cranberry-Raspberry Salad

Serves 8–10

STARTERS

1 pkg. (6 oz.)	raspberry flavored gelatin
3 cups	water
1 can (16 oz.)	whole berry cranberry sauce
1 cup each	celery and red-skinned apple, minced
2/3 cup	walnuts, chopped and divided

CREAMY TOPPING

1 pkg. (8 oz.)	Neufchatel cheese, softened
2 Tblsp.	sugar
1 Tblsp.	lemon juice

GAMEPLAN

In a medium glass bowl, dissolve gelatin in 1-1/2 cups boiling water, stirring until mixture is clear. Stir in 1-1/2 cups cold water. Refrigerate until partially set (about 1 to 1-1/2 hours). Mix together cranberry sauce, celery, apple and fold into thickened gelatin mixture. Reserve 2 tablespoons of walnuts for garnish. Stir remaining walnuts into cranberry raspberry mixture until well blended. Refrigerate several hours until set. Meanwhile prepare Creamy Topping: Beat together cheese, sugar and lemon juice until well blended. When gelatin is set, gently spread topping over salad. Sprinkle with 2 tablespoons of chopped walnuts. Chill until serving time.

MIKE SOLARI

Golden Gate Punch

Serves 1 gallon

S T A R T E R S

1 can (48 oz.)	**pineapple juice**	**1 bottle** (1 qt.)	**sparkling water**
2 cans (12 oz.)	**peach apricot nectar**		**ice**
			raspberries, fresh or frozen
1 can (12 oz.)	**frozen orange juice concentrate**		**fresh mint sprigs**

G A M E P L A N

Combine pineapple juice, nectar, orange juice concentrate and sparkling water in a large punch bowl. Add ice. Garnish with raspberries and mint leaves.

BRONCO HINEK

Goal Post Snack

Makes 2 quarts

S T A R T E R S

1 cup	**M&M's**	**3 cups**	**thin pretzel sticks**
1 cup	**dry roasted peanuts**	**3 cups**	**tiny cheese flavored crackers**
1 cup	**raisins**		

G A M E P L A N

Toss gently in a bowl.

MICHAEL BARNES

California Caesar Salad

Serves 6

S T A R T E R S

1/3 cup	**olive oil**	**1**	**egg,** hard cooked
3 Tblsp.	**fresh lemon juice**	**1**	**large head romaine lettuce,** crisp and washed leaves
2-3 Tblsp.	**anchovy paste or**		
1	**large can anchovies,** drained and chopped		**mushrooms,** sliced
			pine nuts
1 tsp.	**Dijon style mustard**		**croutons,** good quality
1	**large clove garlic,** pressed	**1/4 cup**	**parmesan cheese,** grated
1/4 tsp.	**black pepper**		

G A M E P L A N

Combine oil, lemon juice, anchovy paste or anchovies, mustard, garlic and black pepper. Mix well. Toss with romaine leaves. Add some sliced mushrooms, pine nuts and croutons. Toss again. Grate egg over top. Sprinkle with cheese.

TED WALSH

San Francisco Tossed Salad

Serves 6–8

S T A R T E R S

6 cups	**romaine and escarole lettuce,** chopped	**BLUE CHEESE DRESSING**	
3 cups	**red cabbage,** finely shredded	**1/3 cup each**	**mayonnaise and sour cream**
1 can (8 oz.)	**garbanzo beans,** drained and rinsed	**2 Tblsp.**	**red wine vinegar**
2 cups	**cauliflower,** thinly sliced	**1/4 tsp.**	**pepper**
1/2 cup	**red onion,** thinly sliced	**1/3 cup**	**blue cheese,** crumbled
1/4 cup	**pimiento stuffed olives,** sliced		

G A M E P L A N

Prepare blue cheese dressing: Combine mayonnaise, sour cream, red wine vinegar, pepper and blue cheese. Combine salad ingredients in a large bowl. To serve add dressing and toss.

Cookin' with Champions thanks those 49er alumni who responded to our request and regret that some stars may be missing.

STARTING LINEUP

ALUMNI

SUPER BOWL ERA

"THE CATCH"

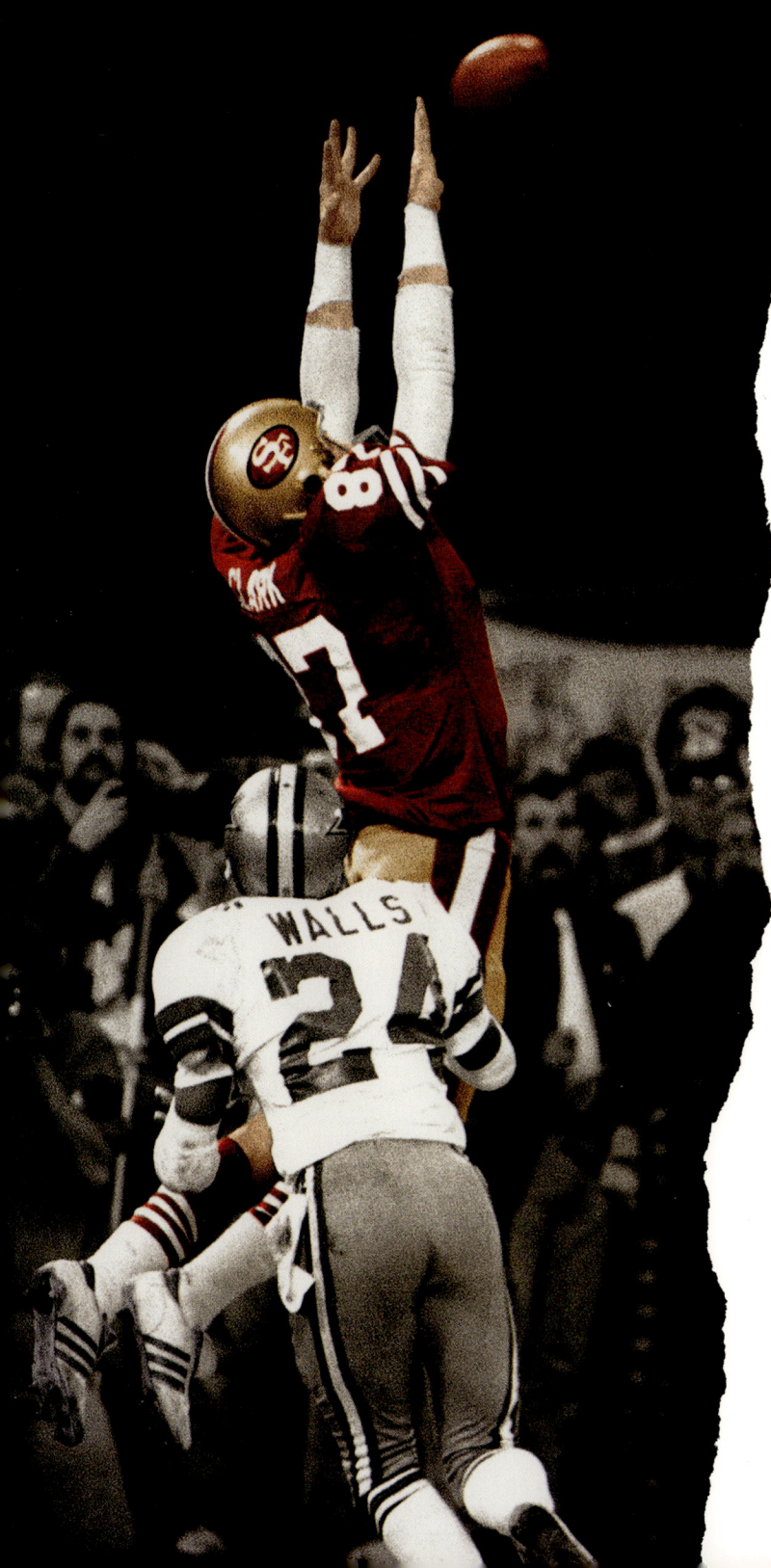

"The Catch"
Montana to Clark
On to Super Bowl XVI

Photo: John Storey
Copyright 1981 • San Francisco Examiner

FRANKIE ALBERT

Winter Fruit Compote

Makes 2 quarts

STARTERS

1 can (16 oz.) · · · · · · · · · · **sliced peaches in light syrup**

1 can (20 oz.) · · · · · · · · **pineapple chunks in juice**

2 · · · · · · · · · · · · · · · · **navel oranges** (grated peel from 1 orange)

2 Tsp. · · · · · · · · · · · · · · · · · · **vanilla**

1 · · · · · · · · · · · · **cinnamon stick** (3 inch)

1 · **small bay leaf**

1/3 cup · · **dried cranberries or raisins**

2 cups · · · · · · · · · · · · · · · **seedless red and green grapes**

1 pkg. (10 oz.) · · · · · **frozen raspberries,** thawed but still icy

2 · · · · · **medium bananas,** peeled and sliced

102

GAMEPLAN

Drain peaches and pineapple, reserve syrup. Combine syrup, grated orange peel, vanilla, cinnamon stick and bay leaf in a medium saucepan. Bring to boil, reduce heat and simmer uncovered for 10 minutes. Remove from heat, add cranberries or raisins. Cool. Peel oranges, removing

seeds if necessary and cut into bite-size chunks. Combine peaches, pineapple, oranges and grapes. Remove cinnamon and bay leaf from syrup. Pour syrup over fruit. Chill. When ready to serve fold in bananas and raspberries.

13 First in long line of great 49er quarterbacks. Stanford grad played with 49ers from 1946-52.

ALUMNI

JOHN BRODIE

Spicy Rice and Pork Lettuce Rolls

Serves 6–8

S T A R T E R S

2	**large eggs,** scrambled
1/2 lb.	**lean ground pork** (loin or tenderloin)
	oil for browning
1 Tblsp.	**fresh ginger,** grated
3 cups	**long grain rice,** cooked
3/4 Tblsp.	**salt**
1/2 cup	**green onion,** thinly sliced
1/2 cup	**cilantro,** chopped
	lettuce leaves, crisp
	hot chili oil to taste

G A M E P L A N

In a medium skillet brown pork and ginger using oil if necessary. Add rice and salt. Heat through, stirring. Fold in onions, cilantro and egg. Spoon onto lettuce leaves: drizzle with chili oil, roll and enjoy.

12 Considered one of the finest pure passers of his era. Another Stanford star who played with 49ers from 1957-73.

ALUMNI

103

ROGER CRAIG
Garden Salad Medley

Serves 8–10

S T A R T E R S

1 cup ····· **carrots,** sliced and lightly cooked

2 cups ··· **broccoli florets and stems,** lightly cooked

2 cups ··········· **cauliflower florets**

2 cups ············· **mushrooms,** sliced

1/2 cup ····· **red pepper,** cut in thin strips

1/4 cup ·········· **pitted Greek olives**

1 ············· **small lemon,** thinly sliced

H E R B   D R E S S I N G

1/3 cup ····················· **olive oil**

1/4 cup ············· **red wine vinegar**

1 ············ **large garlic clove,** pressed

1 tsp. each ············ **sugar and salt**

1/4 tsp. ················ **black pepper**

1 Tblsp. ··············· **fresh dill,** minced or **1 tsp. dried dill**

104

G A M E P L A N

Prepare herb dressing: Combine olive oil, vinegar, garlic, sugar, salt, black pepper and fresh or dried dill. Combine salad ingredients in a shallow glass or stainless steel container. Toss with herb dressing. Chill at least 2 hours, tossing occasionally.

33 High-stepping back from Nebraska played on three Super Bowl teams from 1983-90. First back to gain 1,000 yards rushing and receiving in the same season.

ALUMNI

RANDY CROSS

Crab Meat au Gratin

[snap from wife Patrice]

Serves 6

S T A R T E R S

1/2 cup	butter
1/2 cup	all-purpose flour
2 cups	Half & Half
1 lb.	fresh crab meat
2 Tblsp.	cream sherry
1/2 lb. (8 oz.)	sharp cheddar cheese, grated
	salt and white pepper to taste
	cayenne pepper to taste

S U B S T I T U T E S

	low-fat milk
4-6 oz.	cheese

G A M E P L A N

Preheat oven to 350°F. In top of double boiler melt butter and blend in flour. Gradually add the Half & Half, stirring constantly until the mixture thickens. Add crab meat, salt, white pepper and cayenne pepper, mixing well. Heat thoroughly. Blend in sherry. Pour the mixture into a two quart casserole or individual shells. Top with cheese and bake 20 minutes.

O P T I O N   P L A Y

You can make a low-fat white sauce by using half the butter and low-fat milk. 4-6 oz. of cheese on top should be plenty.

51 Anchor of the offensive line for Team of the Decade; played in three Super Bowls at two different positions.

ALUMNI

105

KEITH FAHNHORST

Reuben Chicken

Serves 4

STARTERS

4 ...... **chicken breasts,** boneless, skinless
1 can (8 oz.) .... **sauerkraut**
4 slices .... **corned beef**
4 slices .... **Swiss cheese**
1/4 tsp. .... **salt**
1/8 tsp. .... **pepper**

THOUSAND ISLAND DRESSING

1 cup .... **mayonnaise**
1/4 cup .... **ketchup**
1/4 tsp. .... **salt**
1/8 tsp. .... **pepper**
1/4 cup .... **sweet relish**
1 Tblsp. .... **onions,** chopped

GAMEPLAN

Put chicken breasts in a greased baking pan and sprinkle with salt and pepper. Cover with well drained sauerkraut. Top with slices of corned beef over slices of Swiss cheese. Cover with this wonderful thousand island dressing as follows: mayonnaise, ketchup, sweet relish, onions, salt and pepper. After pouring the dressing over the chicken cover and bake for 1-1/2 hours at 350°F.

OPTION PLAY

Keeping the corned beef and Swiss cheese portions small will help keep it low-fat. The thousand island dressing is a killer!

71 Huge force at right tackle as offensive line set tone during start of Super Bowl era. Played with 49ers from 1974-87.

ALUMNI

DWIGHT HICKS
"Hot Licks" Barbecue

Serves 4

STARTERS

3 pkgs. ····· **lean pork baby back ribs**

1 cup ············· **teriyaki marinade**

1/2 cup ························ **water**

Kraft Hickory Smoke Barbecue sauce

············· **Bulls Eye Barbecue sauce**
or your favorite sauce

107

GAMEPLAN

Put water and 1/2 of teriyaki marinade into deep roasting pan (the type used for cooking a turkey). Cut ribs into sections of 3 ribs and place into pan. Turn over into marinade as you place ribs. Pour remaining marinade on top of ribs. Cover with foil and bake at 325°F for 1 hour.

22 Led rookie secondary to team's first Super Bowl as safety, then moved to cornerback in championship game three years later.

ALUMNI

Start your barbecue fire after the ribs have cooked 45 minutes. When charcoal is ready, take ribs out of oven and place on barbecue. Put sauce on ribs. Turn ribs and baste again. Cook until the sauce looks done but not burned. Cover ribs to keep hot and serve with baked beans, salad and French bread.

JIMMY JOHNSON

Garlic Chicken Thailand

Serves 5

S T A R T E R S

1 ········ **roasting chicken** (4 lb.), cut into pieces

6 cloves ··············· **garlic,** crushed

2 tsp. ······························· **salt**

1 Tblsp. ··········· **peppercorns,** crushed

2 Tblsp. ················· **lemon juice**

············· **fresh cilantro,** chopped finely

108

G A M E P L A N

Crush the garlic and mix with the salt. Crush the peppercorns coarsely. Wash the cilantro well and finely chop the stems and leaves. Mix all the seasonings together and rub mixture into the chicken pieces. Cover and let stand for at least 1hour, or refrigerate overnight. Place the chicken under the broiler, about 6 inches from the heat. Cook, turning every 5 minutes until the chicken is cooked and the skin is crisp.

37 Hall of Famer considered one of the best—if not the best—cornerback to play in the NFL. Played with 49ers from 1961-76.

ALUMNI

JOHN HENRY JOHNSON

Red Velvet Cake

[hand-off from wife Leona]

Serves 12

STARTERS

2-1/2 cups	flour
1 tsp.	baking soda
2 Tblsp.	cocoa
1/2 tsp.	salt
2	eggs
2 cups	sugar
1-1/2 cups	vegetable oil
1 tsp.	vinegar
1 cup	buttermilk

1 tsp.	vanilla extract
1/2 cup	red food coloring

FROSTING

8 oz.	cream cheese, softened
2 Tblsp. at a time	milk
2 lbs.	powdered sugar
1 Tblsp.	vanilla extract
1/2 cup	walnuts, crushed

GAMEPLAN

Sift together flour, baking soda, cocoa and salt. Combine eggs, sugar, oil and vinegar. Beat well. Add flour mixture alternately with buttermilk, mixing well. Add vanilla and food coloring. Pour into a greased and floured 13 x 9 x 2 sheet pan or two 9-inch round cake pans. Bake at 350°F for 20 to 30 minutes or until the center of cake springs back when touched. Cool on racks for frosting. Cream cheese frosting: combine cream cheese, powdered sugar and vanilla in large bowl. Add milk, 2 tablespoons at a time, until correct consistency. Beat until fluffy. Press crushed walnuts on sides of cake.

35 A quarter of the "Million Dollar Backfield," this Arizona State graduate and Pro-Football Hall of Famer played with the 49ers from 1954–56.

ALUMNI

RONNIE LOTT

Lotta Spicy Pasta
[hand-off from wife Karen]
Serves 6

S T A R T E R S

6	mild Italian link sausages
2 Tblsp.	unsalted butter
1	medium onion, chopped
1-1/2 tsp.	red pepper flakes
2 cans (1lb.)	whole Italian plum tomatoes, include juice
1 cup	vodka
1 cup	whipping cream
1 Tblsp.	tomato paste
1 lb.	penne pasta
1 cup	parmesan cheese, grated
	fresh oregano, for garnish

S U B S T I T U T E S

	low-fat chicken / turkey sausage
1 Tblsp.	olive oil
1 cup	Half & Half or whole milk
1/2 cup	parmesan cheese, grated

110

G A M E P L A N

In large pot bring water to boil, add sausage and cook for 10 minutes. Take out and cool. In sauté pan, cook over medium heat, the onions, butter and red pepper flakes. Then add tomatoes and simmer for one hour. Add sausage and vodka, simmer. Turn heat to high, add cream and tomato paste. Stir. Boil pasta, drain and put in bowl. Spoon all other ingredients on top of pasta. Sprinkle with cheese and oregano.

42 Won four Super Bowl rings as "Joe Montana of the defense" from 1981–90. Certain Hall of Famer known for devastating hits, leadership, versatility and instinct.

O P T I O N   P L A Y

Use low-fat chicken or turkey sausage, 1 Tablespoon of olive oil instead of 2 Tablespoons of butter. Half & Half or whole milk instead of whipping cream. 1/2 cup of parmesan cheese instead of 1 cup. This will cut down on the calories and fat intake. The vodka is optional for taste.

ALUMNI

HUGH McELHENNY
Lasagna Rolls

Serves 4–6

STARTERS

8	lasagna noodles
1 pkg. (10 oz.)	frozen spinach, thawed and chopped
1 cup	parmesan cheese, grated
1-1/2 tsp.	salt
1/4 tsp.	pepper
2 cups	light spaghetti sauce
	mozzarella cheese for topping

111

GAMEPLAN

Cook noodles according to package directions. Drain and rinse under cold water, and drain again. Set aside. Squeeze out as much moisture from the spinach as possible. Stir together spinach, 3/4 cup of parmesan cheese, ricotta cheese, nutmeg, salt and pepper. Spread about 1/4 cup of spinach mixture along the entire length of noodle. Place softened noodles on sides and slightly apart in greased 9 x 13 baking dish. Pour spaghetti sauce over noodles. Bake covered at 350°F for 30–45 minutes and sprinkle remaining parmesan and mozzarella cheese over top.

39 They called this Hall of Famer "The King." An incredible broken field runner, a thing of beauty to watch. The most feared runner in league while with the 49ers from 1952–60.

ALUMNI

LEO NOMELLINI
Lion's Den Popcorn

Makes 3 quarts

STARTERS

2 Tblsp. · · · · · · · · · · · · · · · · · **butter,** melted

2 Tblsp. · · · · · · · · · · · · · · · · · **olive oil**

1/2 tsp. each · · · · · · · · · · **dried oregano and garlic powder**

3 quarts · · · · · **freshly popped popcorn**

1/3 cup · · · · · · **parmesan cheese,** grated

112

GAMEPLAN

Combine butter, olive oil, oregano and garlic powder. Drizzle over warm popcorn, tossing gently. Sprinkle with cheese. Toss again and serve.

AUDIBLE

May be re-heated in a low oven.

73 Leo "the Lion" scared most of his opponents with his ferocious play after coming from the University of Minnesota. The Hall of Famer played with the 49ers from 1950-63.

ALUMNI

R. C. OWENS

"Alley Oop" Holiday Cookies

Makes 4 dozen

STARTERS

1 cup	granulated sugar
1 cup	brown sugar
2/3 cup	cooking oil
2/3 cup	butter
3	eggs
3 1/2 cups	flour
1-1/2 tsp.	baking soda

1 tsp.	salt
1 tsp.	vanilla
1 pkg. (12 oz.)	chocolate chips
	peanut butter morsels or chopped nuts, your choice

SUBSTITUTES

	candied fruit

GAMEPLAN

Mix together granulated sugar, brown sugar, oil, butter and eggs. Sift together flour, baking soda and salt. Slowly mix into egg mixture. Add vanilla and mix well. Stir in chocolate chips. Mix well. Shape into 1" balls and place on greased cookie sheet. Press nuts, peanut butter morsels into the top of the dough balls. Bake at 375°F for 8 to 10 minutes.

OPTION PLAY

Candied fruit on top is lower in fat than nuts or peanut butter morsels.

27 So dominant a receiver from 1957–61 with the 49ers that the game named a catch-phrase after him: Alley Oop.

ALUMNI

113

BUBBA PARIS
Baked Stuffed Spuds

Serves 4

STARTERS

4 .... medium-size baking potatoes

4 Tblsp. .... butter (may use half canola oil)

2 Tblsp. .... Dijon style mustard

2 cups .... mushrooms, sliced

1 bunch ...... green onions, thinly sliced

1/2 to 1 cup ... Gruyere or Monterey Jack cheese, shredded

.... pepper, freshly cracked

.... almonds (optional), toasted sliced

GAMEPLAN

Bake potatoes. In large skillet heat butter until lightly browned. Stir in mustard. Add mushrooms and onions, sauté 3 to 5 minutes, stirring. Slice tops of hot potatoes lengthwise and crosswise. Push open. Top with cheese. Spoon mushroom mixture over top. Add a touch of pepper. To indulge, sprinkle with almonds.

77 Big Bubba held down the left tackle spot for the 49ers during three Super Bowls. Drafted out of Michigan and played from 1982–90.

ALUMNI

JOE PERRY

Perry's Pepper Casserole
[hand-off from wife Donna]
Serves 6

STARTERS

3 ············· **red bell peppers,** chopped

3 ·········· **green bell peppers,** chopped

3 ········· **yellow bell peppers,** chopped

3 ································ **tomatoes**

3 cloves ················ **garlic,** chopped

1/4 cup ················· **fresh parsley**

································· **olive oil**

······················ **salt and pepper**

GAMEPLAN

Slice all peppers in 1/4 inch slices. Halve tomatoes and slice length-wise. Chop garlic cloves (fine), add parsley and 1/2 cup olive oil. Place peppers, parsley, tomatoes and chopped garlic into casserole dish. Add salt and pepper to taste. Pour olive oil over all and toss lightly. Bake an additional 10 minutes. Serve hot as a side dish.

AUDIBLE

Bake ahead. Serve cold with french bread at a tail-gate. A healthy recipe.

34 Hall of Famer "The Jet" was first back to post consecutive, 1,000-yard rushing seasons for the 49ers, whom he played for from 1948–60 and also in 1963.

ALUMNI

FRED QUILLAN

Crab Mold

[hand-off from wife Sue]

Serves 10

STARTERS

1 can (6 oz.) · · · · · · · · · · · · · · · · · · · **crab**

1 pkg. (6 oz.) · · · · · · · · · · · · **cream cheese**

1 envelope · · · · · · · · · · · · · **Knox gelatin**

3 Tblsp. · · · · · · · · · · · · · · · · · · · **water**

1 cup · · · · · · · · · · · · · · · · · **celery,** diced

4 · · · · · · · · · · · · · · **green onions,** chopped

1 cup · · · · · · · · · · · · · · · · · **mayonnaise**

1 can · · · · · **cream of mushroom soup**

SUBSTITUTES

· · · · · · · · · · · · · · · · **low-fat cream cheese**

· · · · · · · · · · · · · · · · **low-fat mayonnaise**

GAMEPLAN

Heat and blend cream cheese with cream of mushroom soup. Mix gelatin with water and add to soup mixture. Add mayonnaise and beat with wisk rapidly. Chill mixture for 15 minutes, wisking every 5 minutes to help cool. Add all remaining ingredients and pour into mold. Chill overnight.

OPTION PLAY

To make this more low-fat you could substitute a low-fat cream cheese and a low-fat mayonnaise. Serve with waverly crackers on a bed of lettuce.

56 Considered the most dominant technician at his position while playing for the 49ers from 1978 -87, the start of the Super Bowl era.

ALUMNI

116

FREDDIE SOLOMON
"Solomon" Gumbo

Serves 8

STARTERS

1 lb.	**chicken breasts,** boneless skinless, cut into bite size pieces
3 cups	**water**
1 cup	**chicken broth**
1 clove	**garlic,** minced
1/4 tsp.	**dried red peppers**
1 cup	**onion,** chopped
1	**bay leaf**
1/8 tsp.	**sage**
1/4 tsp.	**thyme**
2 cups each	**okra** (sliced), **tomatoes** (chopped), **corn**
1/2 tsp.	**salt**
1/4 tsp.	**pepper**
2 cups	**long grain white rice**
2 Tblsp. each	**butter, flour**
1 cup	**chicken broth,** additional

GAMEPLAN

Rinse chicken and place in a large soup pot. Cover with water, add 1 cup broth and bring to a boil. Skim off foam with a slotted spoon, then add garlic, peppers, onion, bay leaf, sage and thyme. Cover and simmer for 20 minutes, skim off any foam. Add okra, tomatoes and corn. Cover and continue to simmer for 20 minutes. Season with salt and pepper. While soup is simmering, cook rice according to package. In another pan, melt butter, add flour and stir over medium heat until golden and bubbly. Add second cup of chicken broth, bring to a boil, reduce heat and wisk until smooth. Add to chicken gumbo and stir to combine. Heat thoroughly. Serve over hot rice in soup bowls.

88 Combined hands and speed to complement Dwight Clark during 49ers' first two Super Bowl titles, then tutored a young receiver named Jerry Rice.

ALUMNI

117

BOB ST. CLAIR
Liver "á la raw"

Serves 1

S T A R T E R S

3 slices · lean bacon

1/4 to 1/3 lb. · calves or chicken liver

· crisp lettuce leaf

· lemon wedges

· Tabasco sauce

· · · · · · · · black pepper to taste, fresh ground

1 · · · · · · · · baked potato with butter or
sour cream topping

1/2 pkg. · · · · · · · · · · · frozen peas, cooked

118

G A M E P L A N

Cook bacon until crisp. Finely chop uncooked liver. To serve, place chopped liver on lettuce leaf. Top with cooked bacon. Season with lemon, Tabasco and pepper.

O P T I O N   P L A Y

Dangerous, only Bob could eat this! Don't try this at home. Serve with baked potato and peas on the side.

79 Hall of Famer was devastating blocker from 1953–64. Played at Kezar stadium in high school, college and pros. Still eats raw meat.

ALUMNI

Y. A. TITTLE

Louisiana Pecan Pie à la mode

Serves 6–8

STARTERS

1 cup ··· **light brown sugar,** firmly packed

1/2 cup ························ **sugar**

1 Tblsp. ························ **flour**

2 ···························· **eggs**

2 Tblsp. ························ **milk**

2 tsp. ························ **vanilla**

2 tsp. ····· **orange peel** (optional), grated

1/2 cup ················ **butter,** melted

1 cup ················ **pecans,** chopped

1 (9 inch) ······· **uncooked pie shell**

SUBSTITUTES

For chocolate pecan pie:

1/3 cup ····· **chocolate chip morsels**

GAMEPLAN

Combine sugars and flour. Beat in eggs, milk, vanilla, orange peel (if desired) and butter. Stir in pecans. Pour into pie shell. Bake in middle of 350°F oven for 35-45 minutes, until set. After 20 minutes cover with foil to prevent edges from getting too brown. Cool.

AUDIBLE

Serve with French vanilla ice cream.

14 This Hall of Famer is another in long line of great 49er quarterbacks. Developed the Alley -Oop pass with R. C. Owens while playing with the 49ers from 1951-60.

ALUMNI

KEENA TURNER
Chicken Fried Rice

Serves 4

S T A R T E R S

1 Tblsp.	**corn oil**
1 Tblsp.	**garlic,** minced
1 Tblsp.	**fresh ginger,** minced
1 cup	**onion,** sliced
1/2 medium head	**Chinese cabbage,** coarsely chopped
3 cups	**long grain white rice,** cooked
1/4 cup	**soy sauce**
1/4 cup	**dry sherry**
1/4 cup	**chicken stock or canned chicken broth**
1 cup	**peas,** cooked
1 cup	**carrots,** coarsely chopped
2	**eggs,** beaten
2 Tblsp.	**scallions,** thinly sliced for garnish
8 oz.	**chicken,** coarsely chopped

120

G A M E P L A N

Heat the oil in a wok or a large skillet. Sauté the garlic, ginger and onion over medium to low heat until soft, about 5 minutes. Add the cabbage and carrots, raise the heat to medium and sauté until limp, about 10 minutes. Stirring constantly. About 5 minutes through, add the chicken. Add the rice, soy sauce, sherry and chicken stock. Cook for 3 minutes, stirring constantly. Add the peas and cook for an additional minute. Make a small hole in the center of the rice mixture and pour the eggs into the hole. Cook the eggs for about 1 minute, stirring with a fork, then gently fold the eggs into the rice. Serve immediately, garnished with the scallions.

58 One of five players to win four Super Bowl rings while becoming the prototype for outside linebackers during the 1980s.

ALUMNI

RAY WERSCHING

Chinese Salad
[snap from wife Chrissy]
Serves 6–8

STARTERS

2 pkg.	**Ramen noodle soup, noodles only**
1 pkg.	**slivered almonds**
1 pkg. (1 oz.)	**sesame seeds**
1/2 cup	**margarine or butter**
1 head	**iceberg lettuce,** chopped
1 bunch	**romaine lettuce,** chopped
5	**green onions,** include green part, chopped
1/2 cup	**vegetable oil**
1/4 cup	**vinegar**
1/2 cup	**sugar**
1/4 cup	**soy sauce**

121

GAMEPLAN

In pan melt butter then brown almonds, sesame seeds and noodles. Put aside and cool until crunchy. Tear lettuce and cut onions. Mix separately oil, vinegar, sugar and soy sauce. Just before serving, put noodle mixture with lettuce. Then toss with dressing.

OPTION PLAY

You could add sliced broiled chicken. Break up noodles while they are in the package to make them small, before browning, otherwise, they may clump.

14 Arguably the most popular player at the start of the 49ers' Super Bowl era because of his reliability on field and sense of humor off of it.

ALUMNI

JAMIE WILLIAMS

7-Up Cake
[pass from wife Charlotte]
Serves 12

S T A R T E R S

3 cups	**flour,** sifted twice
3 cups	**sugar**
1/2 tsp.	**salt**
1/3 cup	**Crisco shortening**
5	**eggs**
2 sticks	**butter**
1 tsp.	**lemon extract**
1 tsp.	**butter extract**
1 tsp.	**vanilla extract**
1 can (8 oz.)	**7-Up**

G A M E P L A N

Beat all ingredients together for 10 minutes. Lightly butter a bundt pan, then dust it with flour. Pre-heat the oven to 300°F. Pour mixture into bundt. Bake until cake begins to pull away from the sides of the pan and feels springy to the touch, about 1-1/2 hours. Set cake aside to cool in the pan. Invert cooled cake onto a serving platter.

81 Arrived with dreadlocks and Spiderman nickname and soon became sage of the 49ers locker room as team headed from one dominant decade to the next.

ALUMNI

CARLTON WILLIAMSON

Shrimp and Asparagus Pasta
[interception from wife Donna]
Serves 4

STARTERS

8 oz.	capellini pasta
1 lb.	shrimp
1/2 lb.	fresh asparagus, cut into 2 inch pieces
1/2-3/4 cups	chicken broth
2-3 cloves	garlic, crushed
2 Tblsp.	olive oil
1 Tblsp.	cornstarch

123

GAMEPLAN

Blanch fresh asparagus and set aside. Sauté crushed garlic in olive oil, add shrimp and stir-fry until opaque. Combine cornstarch with chicken broth and pour over shrimp. Cook until shrimp is pink and sauce begins to thicken, stirring frequently. Cook pasta while preparing the shrimp. Add blanched asparagus. Simmer 1 minute. Toss with pasta and optional spices.

OPTION PLAY

Add a dash of cajun seasoning and/or parmesan cheese.

27 Part of the secondary that helped capture the 49ers' first four Super Bowls. Also known for his hitting ability.

ALUMNI

MIKE WILSON

Italian Tomatoes

Serves 4

STARTERS

1/4 cup	extra virgin olive oil
2 Tblsp.	white wine vinegar
2 tsps.	mild mustard
1 clove	garlic, pressed
1 tsp. each	sugar and salt
1/4 tsp.	black pepper
1/4 cup	basil leaves, shredded
2 Tblsp.	parsley, minced
8	medium garden ripe tomatoes

124

GAMEPLAN

Whisk together oil, vinegar, garlic, sugar, salt and pepper. Stir in basil and parsley. Slice tomatoes and arrange on platter slightly overlapping. Drizzle over dressing. Do not refrigerate.

AUDIBLE

Marvelous with crusty bread.

85 Last of the five players who were members of the 49ers' first four Super Bowl teams. Reliable hands, strong work ethic.

ALUMNI

ERIC WRIGHT

Pesto Pasta

Serves 3–4

STARTERS

3/4 cup	**fresh basil,** chopped
1/2 cup	**fresh parsley,** chopped
1/2 cup	**parmesan cheese,** grated
2 Tblsp.	**walnuts or pine nuts**
2 half cloves	**garlic**
3 Tblsp.	**olive oil**
3 Tblsp.	**butter,** softened

1/4 tsp.	**salt**
1/4 tsp.	**pepper**
6 oz.	**linguine, capellini or penne** cooked

SUBSTITUTES

chicken breasts, skinless sliced

margarine

GAMEPLAN

Combine first 9 ingredients in an electric blender or food processor at high speed until smooth. Cook pasta according to package directions. Toss pesto mixture with pasta and serve immediately.

OPTION PLAY

Replace the butter with margarine. You can add chicken for extra protein if you'd like.

21 Final link to the young secondary at the start of the Super Bowl era. At one point was the best coverage cornerback in the NFL.

ALUMNI

So often people hear about what is wrong with professional sports, but how many times do you hear about an entire team joining in an effort to make a major impact on the lives of others? Even fans of the San Francisco 49ers may be surprised when they learn how much money this book will raise for the American Cancer Society and the 49ers Foundation.

Yet, if you've followed the 49ers and their non-profit fundraising foundation, you'll understand. There is more to the five-time Super Bowl champion 49ers than just playing football. Of course, capturing the Lombardi trophies is what drives everyone at the team complex. And it is that unprecedented status as five-time winners that enables the 49ers to build such a foundation. The foundation is run by Lisa DeBartolo, 25-year-old daughter of the team's owner. Lisa DeBartolo, the eldest of the three DeBartolo daughters, took over the 49ers Foundation in 1994. During that time the organization has raised nearly $500,000 for Bay Area charities. "The public should know the 49ers make a major contribution to the community," Lisa DeBartolo says. "Whenever they do something like this cookbook, they are doing it because they care. The main goal of the 49ers Foundation has been to get the word out, to get donations of any size. Think what a lot of small donations from lots of people can do." Lisa DeBartolo has recently been named the team's Vice President/Director of Community Affairs. The 49ers Foundation is pleased to join hands with the American Cancer Society for this cookbook, and thanks you, the reader, for helping our players support both groups. Just imagine how many more organizations can be helped simply by the purchase of this book.

The 49ers Foundation has donated grants to: The Packard Children's Hospital; Outward Bound; The Center for a New Generation; The United Negro College Fund; Marty Lyons Foundation; The Crippled Children's Society; The ALS Foundation; The Police Athletic League; Crime Prevention, Narcotics, Drugs; The Champs Foundation; The Mission Dolores Restoration Project; San Francisco General Hospital Medical Center; Touchstone Support Network; The Ella Hill Hutch Community Center; The Junior Tennis League; The Institute for Better Health; Joyous Sound Productions; Woodrow Wilson High School; The Oakland Youth Association; The Konocti Girl Scouts; Reed Elementary School; The San Jose Jaycees Foundation; The Child Therapy Institute of Marin County; Harrison House; Polynesian Community Services; The Second Harvest Food Bank; Good News Tenderloin Center and The Okizu Foundation.

The 49ers Foundation is a tax-exempt organization under section 501 (c) (3) of the Internal Revenue Service and accepts written requests for grants from public charities. All charitable groups submitting applications must be exempt from taxation under Section 501 (c) (3) of the Internal Revenue Code. Grant requests should be at least two pages and include: A brief description of the organization; what project will be funded through the grant; and who the other major funders are. Also, please enclose a copy of an IRS determination letter granting tax-exempt status. Letters must be submitted between January 1 and April 30. Send request to Lisa DeBartolo, Director, 49ers Foundation, c/o San Francisco 49ers, 4949 Centennial Boulevard, Santa Clara, CA 95054.

LISA DEBARTOLO

Lisa's Ginger Prawns

[pictured on front cover]

Serves 4

S T A R T E R S

1/4 cup ····························· **oil**

2 Tblsp. ····················· **lime juice**

1 Tblsp. each ··· **shallots and parsley,**
chopped

1 Tblsp. ······· **fresh ginger,** finely grated

1/2 tsp. ··············· **lime peel,** grated

12 ····················· **jumbo prawns**
(6 to 7 per pound, tail intact), shelled and de-veined

127

G A M E P L A N

Combine first 5 ingredients. Add prawns, stir to coat. Refrigerate (covered) 1 to 2 hours. Using bamboo or metal skewers, thread 3 prawns on a skewer, securing each prawn at two places. Reserve marinade. Barbecue or broil prawns on grill 6 inches from heat source. Cook, basting with marinade until prawns are pink, turning once.

Graduate of St. Mary's (California) College. Third year with the club after getting firsthand experience in her family's businesses. During her tenure with the 49ers Foundation initiated and managed fund-raisers and special events raising $500,000 for Bay Area charities.

YEH!

KNOW YOUR OPPONENT

128

Any coach will tell you: A high-fat diet can increase your risk of certain cancers. So, here's the game plan: Eat less fat and more vegetables and fruit. And, in case you need a half-time adjustment, here's a pop quiz:

Q Two percent milk has 2% of its calories from fat?

A The label on 2% milk gives the percentage of fat by weight not by calories. Two percent milk is 2% by weight, but is 35% fat by calories. Percentage of calories from fat is a better indicator of the product's nutritional contribution to your diet.

MISSION STATEMENT

The American Cancer Society is the nationwide community-based voluntary health organization, dedicated to eliminating cancer as a major health problem by preventing cancer, saving lives from cancer and diminishing suffering from cancer through research, education, advocacy and service.

AMERICAN CANCER SOCIETY

Q A food labeled "no cholesterol" is also low in fat?

A A product labeled "no cholesterol" or "cholesterol free" does not tell you anything about the fat content. A food can be high in fat and also be cholesterol free. Vegetable oil is an example.

Q Light olive oil has less fat than regular olive oil?

A Light olive oil has the same amount of fat and calories as regular olive oil. It is lighter only in color and tastes milder.

KNOW YOUR OPPONENT

Q Low-fat, low-cholesterol diets are more important for men than women?

A Low-cholesterol, low-fat diets are as important for women as for men. Both are encouraged to cut back on fat in their diets to reduce the risk of heart disease, certain cancers and obesity.

Q You can reduce the fat in cooking by substituting canola oil for butter?

A Oil and butter both contain the same amount of fat—about 12 grams of fat and 110 calories per tablespoon. Use a non-fat cooking spray to keep your foods from sticking.

SAVE LIVES

The American Cancer Society programs of research, education, advocacy and patient services are funded through your contributions. The need for greater funding and participation is urgent. Volunteers and donations are vital to help fight this disease that affects the lives of 3 out of 4 families. There is much yet to accomplish. Your planned gifts and bequests can be a painless way of giving. Please help us attain our goal. For information about the American Cancer Society call 800-ACS-2345.

Q Skinning poultry before cooking can cut the fat content by more than one-half?

A A chicken breast with skin has 15 grams of fat, whereas a chicken breast without the skin has only 6 grams of fat.

Q Eating more fruits and vegetables will reduce the fat in your diet?

A Fruits and vegetables, except for avocado and coconut, are fat free. Fruits and vegetables can reduce the fat in your diet by satisfying your hunger.

KNOW YOUR OPPONENT

Q A large bran muffin is higher in fat than an English muffin sandwich with egg, cheese and ham?

A A large bran muffin has about 13 grams of fat. An English muffin sandwich with egg, cheese and ham has about 11 grams of fat.

Q Hamburgers are always high in fat and should be avoided?

A Hamburgers can be low-fat if they are made with "lean" or "extra-lean" beef, cooked without added fats and topped with lettuce, tomato and pickles instead of cheese and mayonnaise.

LISTEN TO THE COACH

Unless you are under 2 years of age or following a special diet recommended by your doctor, listen to the coach and eat smart:

• Maintain a desirable body weight.
• Eat a varied diet.
• Include a variety of both vegetables and fruits in your daily diet.
• Eat more high-fiber foods, such as whole grain cereals, legumes, vegetables and fruits.
• Cut down on total fat intake.
• Limit consumption of alcoholic beverages.
• Limit consumption of salt-cured, smoked and nitrite-preserved foods.

Q Green salads are always a low-fat choice?

A While green salads are an excellent menu choice, cheese, croutons, bacon bits and creamy salad dressing can add more than 45 grams of fat and 400 calories.

Q The average American consumes the equivalent of a stick of butter every day?

A We need only one tablespoon of fat daily. Unfortunately, the average American consumes the equivalent of 8 tablespoons of fat each day. Eight tablespoons of fat equals one stick of butter.

KNOW YOUR OPPONENT

131

Q A low-fat alternative to chocolate is a carob bar?

A Carob bars usually contain as much fat as chocolate. If you must eat chocolate, cut your favorite bar into bite-size pieces and keep them in the freezer. One piece will take about five minutes to thaw in your mouth, hopefully reducing your craving.

Q If a product is labeled "fat-free," it is safe to assume that there is no fat in it?

A "Fat-free" just means that there is no more than half a gram of fat in the serving listed on the label. This usually works out to one gram of fat in a realistic serving.

VETERAN TECHNIQUES

Your daily calories from fat should not exceed 30% of your total caloric intake. Try to eat no more than 3 grams of fat per 100 calories of food. This translates to less than 50 grams of fat per day for women and 60 grams of fat per day for men.

- Instead of high-fat snacks like nuts and potato chips, try unbuttered popcorn, pretzels or dry cereals (except granolas).
- Make fresh fruits and vegetables your primary snack foods.
- Use non-fat yogurt to replace sour cream or mayonnaise in recipes.
- Instead of eating fried foods, choose those that are broiled, baked, grilled, roasted, stewed or braised.

Q Non-dairy frozen desserts are usually fat-free?

A One-half cup of soy-bean based dessert contains about 11 grams of fat—about the same as super premium ice cream. Read the label.

Q Crackers are a low-fat snack food?

A In many cases, even if they are "baked, not fried," they only look low-fat. Look for crackers which contain less than one gram of fat per ounce.

NFL Record
127th touchdown
by Jerry Rice